ELECTRONICS

Klystron used in radar
system (1950s)

PC hard disk

Mirror galvanometer
(1920s)

Power relay

Satellite receiving
dish (1992)

Interference
suppressor
capacitor

Signal transistor

DK EYEWITNESS BOOKS

ELECTRONICS

Written by
ROGER BRIDGMAN

Audio output transformer

Spectrum of a pulse signal

PC memory board

Small
packaged
integrated
circuit

Silicon chips

Pocket computer
(1990s)

BBC-Marconi
AXBT ribbon
microphone
(1950s)

Dorling Kindersley

Print-out of a pattern
for an integrated circuit

Dorling Kindersley

LONDON, NEW YORK, AUCKLAND, DELHI, JOHANNESBURG,
MUNICH, PARIS and SYDNEY

For a full catalog, visit

 www.dk.com

Project editor Charyn Jones
Art editor Ron Stobbart
Designer Helen Diplock
Production Louise Daly
Managing editor Josephine Buchanan
Managing art editor Lynne Brown
Picture research Deborah Pownall
Special photography Clive Streeter
Editorial consultant Eryl Davies,
Science Museum, London
US editor Charles A. Wills
US consultant Professor Warren Yasso,
Teachers College, Columbia University

Headphones (1920s)

This Eyewitness ® Book has been conceived by
Dorling Kindersley Limited and Editions Gallimard

Published in the United States by
Dorling Kindersley Publishing, Inc.
375 Hudson Street,
New York, NY 10014
6 8 10 9 7 5

Vacuum tube
(1960s)

Dorling Kindersley books are available at special discounts for bulk
purchases for sales promotions or premiums. Special editions, including
personalized covers, excerpts of existing guides, and corporate imprints can
be created in large quantities for specific needs. For more information,
contact Special Markets Dept., Dorling Kindersley Publishing, Inc.

First microphone, made
by David Hughes in 1878

Thyristor for
power control

BTY79

Library of Congress Cataloging-in-Publication Data
Bridgman, Roger.
Electronics / written by Roger Bridgman.
p. cm. — (Eyewitness Books)
Includes index.
1. Electronics — Juvenile literature. [1. Electronics.]
I. Title. II. Series.
QD35.N43 2000
540—dc20   92-54480
                                                            CIP
                                                            AC

ISBN-13: 978-0-7894-6724-9 (ALB)
ISBN-13: 978-0-7894-5598-7 (PLC)

Color reproduction by Colourscan, Singapore
Printed in China by Toppan Printing Co. (Shenzhen) Ltd.

Hand-held video game

Loudspeaker for use with
a radio (1920s)

Contents

Large electromagnet used with the first
magnetron for radar (p. 40)

What is electronics?

Electronic devices can make sounds, send messages, show pictures, measure, remember, calculate, and control. Machines made from wheels and levers can do some of these things, but they are often too slow and clumsy to do them well. Electricity can be used to power such machines, but this does not make them electronic. A machine can claim this title only if it contains devices in which the motion of the tiny particles called electrons that form electric currents can be directly influenced by electricity or magnetism. Devices of this kind allow electricity to control electricity itself. In a television set, for example, electricity from the antenna controls the currents that paint pictures on the screen (pp. 44-45). In a computer, electrical changes caused by pressing keys control the power that writes data to a disk. Using electricity in this way makes it possible to do complicated things quickly and inexpensively. Ordinary machines are good for simple, repetitive jobs like drilling holes or drying hair. But if you want a versatile machine that can instantly change its behavior in response to incoming information, you need electronics. A device like a radio can make a limitless range of sounds, and a powerful electronic computer can conjure up an infinity of imaginary worlds.

THE MANUAL ADDING MACHINE
Until the 1940s the word computer meant a person, not a machine. Because electronic systems can read, write, and apply simple rules, they have claimed much of the work that used to be done by hundreds of clerks toiling in large offices. The actor Tony Hancock satirized this existence in the 1961 film *The Rebel*.

ELECTROMECHANICAL TELEPHONE
The telephone has been a vital part of communications for more than a century, and both electrical and electronic techniques have played a part in its development. The traditional instrument is electric, not electronic. It includes nothing that can control electricity electrically. To dial, a disk is rotated, winding up a spring that operates moving contacts to signal numbers to the exchange. Incoming calls are signaled by a hammer, moved by electromagnets, hitting a pair of bells. There is no memory. Speech is amplified (pp. 30-31) by the microphone inside the handset (pp. 42-43). Telephones of this type are the direct descendants of instruments designed in the 19th century, long before electronics was thought of, but they are still in service all over the world.

Switch hook opens line circuit when handset is replaced

Handset cord

Hand wiring

Terminal

Resistor

Electromagnet

Rotary dial

Handset

Bell

Quartz crystal for frequency control

Filter removes unwanted signals

Integrated circuit processes radio signals

Loudspeaker *Keyboard* *Percussion pad*

MAKING MUSICAL SOUNDS

Every musical instrument has a characteristic sound that depends on the frequencies (pp. 14-15) it produces and the way its notes start and stop. Once a sound has been analyzed, electronic devices can mimic it by using oscillators, amplifiers, and filters (pp. 34-35). Notes from actual instruments can be recorded in electronic memory and be retrieved and manipulated using a keyboard. Electronic circuits allow musicians to produce sounds that never existed before.

RADIO PAGER

Except for large organizations like the police, keeping in touch electronically started with the radio pager, or beeper, which merely listens out for its own call sign and beeps when it detects it. In the 1970s even a simple gadget like this was rare. Today's sophisticated technology makes them available to most everyone.

HEART MONITOR

Muscles like the heart produce electrical effects when they work. Electronics can make this activity visible to doctors. The electrocardiograph amplifies and records electrical signals from the heart, picked up by contacts on the patient's body – just one of the many medical applications of electronics.

Switch hook opens line circuit when handset is replaced

ELECTRON MICROGRAPH

Electronics is about controlling fundamental electrical particles called electrons (pp. 26-27). One thing electrons do is form magnified images. Electrons can show far smaller details than the light used by ordinary microscopes. This color-enhanced picture was made by scanning the subject with a beam of electrons.

A flea magnified 30 times

Printed circuit board

Printed circuit board

Keypad

ELECTRONIC TELEPHONE

Modern telephones are truly electronic. They use electrical control devices called transistors (pp. 38-39), as well as oscillators (pp. 32-33) to signal numbers by generating tones when the keys are pressed. An oscillator and transducer (pp. 42-43) replace the heavy bells of older telephones, giving the distinctive warbling sound of the electronic telephone. The last number dialed is held in an electronic memory (pp. 56-57), and an electronic amplifier boosts the small signal coming from a lightweight microphone. The components are built into the printed circuit boards.

Handset

The pre-electric world

GUIDING SPEECH
Normal speech has limited range because it spreads out in all directions, wasting most of its power. But sound can be channeled through tubes over short distances. Large houses used to have speaking tubes to direct the power to where it was needed, usually from the family's quarters to the servants' quarters.

Aᴿᴼᵁᴺᴰ 1840 ᴇʟᴇᴄᴛʀɪᴄɪᴛʏ ꜱᴛᴀʀᴛᴇᴅ ᴛᴏ ᴄʜᴀɴɢᴇ the way people live. Messages from the electric telegraph (pp. 24-25) began to replace letters brought by horse or ship. Electric power followed soon after. Machines to help people communicate with each other, control things, and do calculations have existed for a long time. In these simple machines lie the beginnings of some basic ideas used in electronics – principles like logic, amplification, and memory. The machines worked slowly and cost a lot to build and run. Many broke down, and their ropes, levers, or wheels wore out in time. Communication devices were primitive. At night you could signal yes or no by lighting or not lighting a fire. This idea of a code based on just two possibilities lives on today at the heart of every digital electronic system.

Millions row

Black bead helps counting

ANCIENT CALCULATOR
The abacus is an elegant calculating aid that probably originated in ancient Babylon. The beads of this Russian abacus, or *stchoty*, are designed to count money. The top row counts millions, the next hundreds of thousands, and so on. Expert users can often beat an electronic calculator to the correct answer.

STEERING A TRUE COURSE
The person at the helm of this oceangoing yacht watches the compass and uses the rudder to correct any deviation from the desired course. The helm acts as an amplifier, feeding back information from the compass to control the mighty power of wind and sea.

Quarters row

Frame

Rope controlling pull

Cylinder

Steam valve

Brake handle

Connecting rod

Drum

AMPLIFYING A SIGNAL
Capstans are used to move heavy weights by means of ropes or chains. They are turned continuously by powerful engines, but will not pull on a load until the rope is tightened around the drum by a much gentler pull from its operator. In the same way, although an audio amplifier is plugged into the electrical output all the time, power only reaches the speakers under the control of a tiny signal from something like a compact disc player.

FEEDING BACK INFORMATION
This American wind-powered water pump of 1888 uses simple principles to keep it under control. The steering vane at the back keeps the whole mechanism facing the wind by means of a rudimentary feedback system (pp. 30-31). Any deviation from the correct direction causes unbalanced wind pressures on the two sides of the vane, which pushes it in the direction needed to correct the error. Another mechanism controls the speed and prevents the mill from being damaged by high winds. As the wind blows harder, the blades on the wheel tilt until the push of the wind balances the push of a counterweight. This keeps the pump going at a fairly constant speed.

Steering vane

Operating lever

Tower

Blades

PICKING A LOCK
Locks combine logic (pp. 50-51) and memory (pp. 56-57) by comparing an internal pattern with the pattern of a key, and only opening if the two match. Combination locks do not use a key – their secret pattern of numbers is stored in the brain of their owner. But sometimes burglars can guess the pattern by listening to the sound as the notches line up.

MECHANICAL COMMUNICATION
People can sometimes communicate at a distance by waving their arms. French engineer Claude Chappe (1763-1805) put giant mechanical arms and telescopes on hilltop towers and used a special code (pp. 48-49) to bring news of a French victory from the Austrian border to Paris in less than an hour.

CHARLES BABBAGE (1791-1871)
Before electronics, tables were used to aid calculation. Babbage, a British mathematician, designed several machines to generate error-free tables for navigation. None of the machines was completed in his lifetime.

RAILWAY SIGNALS
Remote communication was difficult before electricity. The only signals that could travel far used light, and that usually meant either daylight on semaphore arms or oil lamps shining through colored glass. But signals like these on a railway line were a reliable way of communicating simple stop-go instructions to a moving vehicle. Mechanical logic interlocked signals and switches for added safety.

Rope pulling load

Counterweight

Shaft conveys power to water pump

Electricity and magnetism

ELECTRICITY AND MAGNETISM are closely intertwined. Two of the greatest discoveries of the 19th century were that a wire carrying an electric current acts like a magnet and a change of magnetism can make current flow. (This also means that a changing current in one wire can make current flow in another.) These discoveries have had an enormous effect on everyday life. They have allowed us, for example, to build generators that convert the energy in fuels like coal or oil into abundant electric power, using wires with currents flowing in them as magnets and whirling them past other wires to create even bigger currents. Just a little of this power goes into electronic devices. By exploiting the intimate relationship between magnetism and electricity, electronic devices can make music, pictures, or even radio waves.

PIONEER OF ELECTRICITY
Michael Faraday (1791-1867) rose from a poor family to become one of the greatest scientists of his day. Working in London at the Royal Institution, he made many fundamental discoveries in chemistry and physics. In 1831, having read about the work of Hans Christian Oersted (p. 11), he discovered that changing magnetism near a wire causes current to flow. This completed the link between magnetism and electricity.

Permanent magnet

Pulley to spin motor quickly

Wire wound on armature

Light bulb

Generator

MEASURING CURRENT
Tangent galvanometers used Oersted's discovery to measure current. The instrument was turned until the coil pointed the same way as the compass needle. Current passing through the coil then created magnetism at right angles to the magnetism of the Earth. As the needle swung to a new angle, it showed the strength of the current. This galvanometer was made in Britain in about 1900.

Small magnet for fine adjustment

Electric motor

Battery

Commutator reverses current in wires as armature rotates

Permanent magnet

Wire wound on armature

Short compass needle

Coil

Connecting terminal

Scale graduated in degrees

THE MOTOR AND GENERATOR
An electric motor normally converts electrical energy into mechanical work. With a battery connected to the motor, currents in the wires create magnetism that pushes against the permanent magnet, making the armature spin and turning the handle. If the battery is replaced by a bulb and the handle turned to spin the armature, the motor becomes a generator. Currents induced as the wires move past the magnet make the bulb light up. As Faraday realized, there is an interplay between electricity and magnetism.

USING ELECTRICITY AND MAGNETISM
Like a television set, a video cassette recorder (VCR) receives signals from a television station or cable. But instead of turning signals into pictures, the VCR stores them on magnetic tape. The process is much the same as recording sound (pp. 52-53). The VCR relies heavily on magnetism and electricity. It uses the magnetic push of current-carrying wires in an electric motor to spin a drum at high speed and move the tape slowly past it. To record a program, currents flowing through coils of wire inside the drum create magnetic patterns on the tape. When the tape is played back, the VCR uses these magnetic patterns to produce currents that a television set can turn into pictures.

Video cassette recorder (late 1970s)

Spreading the word

Without Hans Christian Oersted's famous observation of 1820, electricity and magnetism might have remained separate and mysterious subjects. Oersted published his findings in 1821, enabling Michael Faraday (p. 10) and later James Maxwell (p. 12) to do the work that led to electric power and the discovery of radio waves. Joseph Henry (pp. 18-19) used Oersted's work to understand how magnetic components such as inductors behave. Building on this, Oliver Heaviside (p. 13) explained how electric signals travel through long cables. This extended the speed and range of international communication.

HANS CHRISTIAN OERSTED (1777-1851)
Oersted was a Danish scientist whose discoveries linked magnetism to electricity and pointed physics toward a deeper understanding of these subjects. But scientists of his day did not always stick to one science. Oersted was the first person to prepare aluminum as a pure metal. He also isolated piperine, the chemical that makes pepper peppery.

Angle of needle can increase to 90° with strong enough current

Terminal connecting to battery

Loop of wire

Terminal

Wooden base

Magnetic compass needle

OERSTED'S COMPASS
Lecturing at the University of Copenhagen in 1820, Oersted connected a battery to a wire that happened to run near the needle of a compass. The magnetic needle swung around, and Oersted immediately realized the significance. The current-carrying wire was acting as a magnet and revealed that magnetism and electricity were related.

Erase head prepares tape for new recording

Angled, spinning drum carrying two record/playback heads

Tape records pictures as magnetic stripes

Sound record/playback head

Capstan rotates to feed tape past drum

Motor driven by pulses that keep drum in step with pictures

Electromagnetic waves

WAVES ARE ALL AROUND US, rippling on water, rolling across a field of corn or keeping a centipede's legs organized – and bringing us sound and light. Waves allow something to go from one place to another without anything moving very much, making them of vital importance to communication. Waves usually occur in a medium that can store and pass on energy in two different but related forms. Sound, for instance, can travel in anything able to store energy as motion and pressure. For electromagnetic waves the medium is space itself, which can store energy in electric and magnetic form. Scottish mathematician James Clerk Maxwell (1831-1879) extended the work done by Michael Faraday (p. 10). He realized that the close relationship between electricity and magnetism make this kind of wave possible. His calculations showed that the wave would travel at the speed of light, making him suspect that light itself was an electromagnetic wave. In 1888, Heinrich Hertz generated waves electrically and showed that they behave just like light, confirming Faraday's and Maxwell's ideas.

PROVING WAVES EXIST
In 1886, at Karlsruhe in Germany, physicist Heinrich Hertz (1857-1894) set out to see if Maxwell was right about the existence of radio waves. He made high-voltage sparks jump between two rods and noticed that tiny sparks jumped across a gap between two other rods some distance away, suggesting that electromagnetic waves were crossing the room. Using flat and curved reflectors, wooden prisms, and many other devices, Hertz was able to show that the waves behave very much like light.

WAVE MACHINE
There are two ways of looking at a wave: either focusing on a fixed point or following the shape of the wave as it travels. Every point goes through the same cycle of changes, but a point a little farther from the source of the wave goes through its cycle a little later. The wave shape is the combined effect of all the points doing the same thing slightly out of step. This model demonstrates wave motion using pivoted slats linked by springs. As each slat swings, it stretches a spring, moving the next slat. The speed of the wave depends on the properties of the slats and springs, just as the speed of electromagnetic waves is governed by the electric and magnetic properties of space.

WAVES MAKING THINGS HAPPEN
When a metal disk strikes a closely packed and firmly held line of disks, a loose one at the far end shoots off. A pressure wave in the metal, traveling much faster than the moving disk, carries its energy down the line. In a similar way, when a bulb is connected to a battery, an electromagnetic wave tells the bulb to start glowing long before any electrons from the battery get there.

Hand supplies energy to wave

Metal slats swing, storing energy, as springs relax

Pivot wire

Wooden frame

Copper parabolic reflector

Spark gap

Ebonite supporting rods

Spark gap

HOW THE TRANSMITTER WORKS

With a simple wire antenna, energy radiates in all directions. Only a little of it reaches the distant detector or receiver. By using a reflector at the transmitter, the waves can be shaped so that less power is wasted.

Reflected waves focused into parallel beam

Some waves are not reflected so they spread out

MARCONI TRANSMITTER

In 1894, Italian scientist Guglielmo Marconi (1874-1937) began experimenting with electromagnetic waves. Imitating Hertz, he experimented with waves concentrated by a curved reflector. This 1896 beam transmitter succeeded in sending signals more than 2 miles (3 km).

Electromagnetic waves transmitted from here

Small balls feed electricity to spark gap

Plastic tube

WAVE GUIDES

One way of sending waves where they are needed is to use a pair of wires. This does not work at high frequencies, for example in satellite communications. Metal or metal-lined tubes called waveguides can be used instead.

Copper wire

OLIVER HEAVISIDE (1850-1925)

The British mathematician and physicist Oliver Heaviside realized that information travels along a cable as a wave in the space between the conductors, rather than through the conductors themselves. His mathematical concepts made it possible to design long-distance telephone cables. He also discovered why radio waves bend around the Earth. This led to long-range radio reception.

SATELLITE GROUND STATION

Radio signals can be directed towards a satellite hovering 22,000 miles (35,000 km) above the Earth, much as a flashlight can be shined on something in the dark. The same dish can also concentrate the faint waves from the distant satellite to give clear reception.

Springs stretch, storing energy, as slats slow down

Green strips show up wave shape

The importance of frequency

ELECTROMAGNETIC WAVES go through a continual cycle of changing electricity and magnetism. Any pattern or wave that repeats in this way has a frequency – the number of repeats per second – and every radio dial shows how important frequency is in electronics. Equally important are the changing shapes of waves, which enable them to carry information. Electronics engineers deal with the infinite variety of possible shapes by describing them in terms of a limited range of frequencies. A wave of any shape can be thought of as a combination of simpler waves of a standard shape. The recipe listing the frequencies, strengths, and relative timing of the waves making up a particular shape is called its spectrum. Breaking complex waves down into their basic ingredients like this makes it much easier to understand and design electronic systems.

Operator uses pointer to trace wave shape

HENRICI'S HARMONIC ANALYZER
The procedure for finding spectra mathematically is simple but tedious – ideal work for a machine. Several were designed in the 19th century. They all rely on someone using a pointer attached to the mechanism to trace the shape of the wave to be analyzed. This one, designed by Professor Olaus Henrici (1840-1918), uses the motions of three glass balls that turn numbered dials. When the whole curve has been traced, the readings of these dials indicate the shape of the wave's spectrum.

REGULAR WAVES
Baron Joseph Fourier (1768-1830) was a French mathematician and an expert on Egypt – he went there with Napoleon in 1798. His method of analyzing waves, published in 1822, was a spin-off of his work on the flow of heat. It shows how any wave can be built up from simpler waves. This powerful branch of mathematics has contributed to important modern developments like electronic speech recognition.

One cycle of wave previously drawn on paper

Center line

Pulley system turned by wire as pointer moves

Glass ball

Dial rotates and numbers are read off dial

Wheel rolls as pointer follows wave

14

SINE WAVE
This smooth, simple curve is called a sine wave. Using Fourier's method, more complex waves are analyzed into this basic shape. The wave is displayed by an oscilloscope, an instrument that produces a graph showing how voltage varies with time. Harmonic oscillators (pp. 32-33) of all kinds generate an output like this.

SINE WAVE SPECTRUM
Most waves can be thought of as made from several sine waves of different frequencies. A spectrum analyzer, used to display this picture, is an instrument that produces a graph showing how much of each frequency is present. A pure sine wave contains only one frequency, which shows up on the analyzer as a single peak.

PULSES
Pulses are on-off signals, reproduced here from an oscilloscope screen. Simple, repeated pulses like these can be used for timing in clocks, television, or computers. More complicated pulse sequences can form a code (pp. 46-49) to represent information in computers and communication systems.

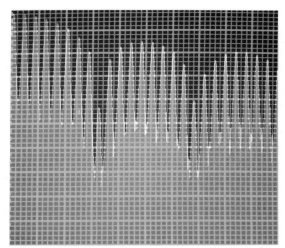

PULSE SPECTRUM
Although these pulses repeat at a similar frequency to the sine wave (above left), their sharp, narrow shape means that they also contain a large number of higher frequency components. These show up on the spectrum analyzer screen as a characteristic pattern of peaks.

SWINGING OF A PENDULUM
The Italian astronomer Galileo Galilei (1564-1642) observed that pendulums swing at a constant frequency and so can be used to make clocks. Knowing the number of ticks per second, it is only necessary to count the ticks to keep track of time. Galileo designed his pendulum clock in 1642, but this one was built in 1883 from drawings of Galileo's clock. Quartz clocks use the same idea of constant frequency, although the quartz crystal vibrates at a much higher frequency than a pendulum.

LIGHT SPECTRUM
Our eyes respond only to the frequency and intensity of light waves, not their shape. When white light is split into its components, as in this hologram, the highest frequencies register as violet and the lowest as red. The simple way the eye analyzes light allows any color to be matched using just three frequencies. This makes color television (pp. 44-45) possible.

Resistors

In ELECTRONICS, RESISTANCE PROVIDED BY RESISTORS plays the part of friction. Friction is sometimes a nuisance, but life would be difficult without it – wheels and feet would not grip the road, brakes would not stop cars, things would slide out of control. Without resistance, there would be a similar lack of control in electronic circuits. Electric currents are caused by the voltages that arise when there are different amounts of electricity in different parts of a circuit. When such a voltage starts to drive current through a resistor, an opposing voltage is generated between its ends, pushing against the driving voltage and limiting the current. This effect is sometimes used directly, for example to prevent light-emitting diodes (pp. 44-45) from burning out. More often, the voltages set up by currents in resistors like to convey information or to help other components such as transistors (pp. 38-39) do their job. Like brakes and clutches, their frictional equivalents in machines, resistors get hot when they work because they exert control by wasting power as heat. They can only reduce the power of an electrical signal, never increase it.

OHM'S LAW
German physicist Georg Simon Ohm (1787-1854) found that the current in a conductor is always equal to the voltage between its ends, divided by a fixed number, its resistance. The unit of resistance – the ohm, indicated by the symbol Ω – is named after him.

Cable controls pressure of brake block on wheel

BRAKING
The speed of a bicycle coasting downhill is limited by friction, which produces a force opposing gravity and increases with speed. When friction balances gravity, the bike stops accelerating. Resistors can control current from a battery by producing opposing voltages that increase with current. When the power is switched on, current increases until the resistor voltages balance the battery voltage.

Brake block rubs against wheel to control friction

Terminal

Bypass plug

NALDER BRO & C°. LONDON   N° 4991   RIGHT AT1.. °C

MEASURING RESISTANCE
Two voltage dividers (p. 17) connected to one battery measure resistance in this 19th-century circuit, known as a Wheatstone bridge. The resistor to be measured and a resistor with a known value make one divider; two more known resistors form the other. When the divider voltages are equal, so that a meter bridging them reads zero, the resistor ratios in both dividers must be the same, giving the value of the unknown resistor. Modern instruments use the same principle.
To use this bridge, the unknown resistor, battery, and meter are connected to terminals. Resistors inside the box are brought into play by pulling out plugs that normally bypass them.

Accurate resistor

Unknown resistor

Accurate resistor

Meter

Arrow shows direction and strength of current

Battery

Accurate resistor

Redness indicates voltage

Principle of Wheatstone bridge

First resistor (22 ohm)

First resistor voltage

3.6 V

VOLTAGE DIVIDER
Many electronic circuits are supplied with power at only one voltage. Different voltages may be needed in some places. The potential divider circuit is one way of getting a smaller voltage from a larger one. The total voltage across the resistors is equal to the battery voltage (here it is 9 volts), but because there are two resistors, this gets split into two smaller voltages proportional to the resistor values. A voltage divider is also known as a potentiometer.

9.0 V

Battery voltage

5.4 V

Second resistor voltage

Second resistor (33 ohm)

Voltage

Battery

Groove cut by laser to adjust resistance

Glass or ceramic tube

Metal film

End cap

Wire

DIFFERENT TYPES OF RESISTORS
It takes work to force current through a resistor. This makes the resistor hot – how hot depends on its size and shape, so there are different resistors for different power levels, each with a maximum wattage rating. (The resistors are shown here approximately actual size.) There are special resistors for high frequencies (pp. 40-41) and for digital circuits (pp. 46-47). There are also variable resistors, usually made as potential dividers or potentiometers, so that voltages can be scaled down at will.

RESISTOR CONSTRUCTION
Many resistors are made from a glass or ceramic tube coated with a thin film of metal. A laser trims the resistor to its correct value by burning away some of the metal. Resistors can also be made using carbon or from resistive wire. In most cases, end caps and wires are added to make the connections, and the body is painted. The colored stripes indicate the resistance value and accuracy of the resistor.

STAYING IN STEP
A good resistor obeys Ohm's law even if the voltage or current varies rapidly. The two wavy lines on this picture, displayed by an oscilloscope (p. 33), show current through a resistor staying exactly in step with the voltage as it goes up and down.

Current in step with voltage

1/8th-watt resistor used for signal and data circuits

2-watt resistor for small power-supply circuits

A potentiometer used for graphic equalizers

472

Chip resistor

A potentiometer used for volume and tone controls

Pre-set resistor used inside television sets

185-166
100W 47R ±5% 92-26

SPEED ON ICE
Skaters use controlled friction in two ways. At first, the blades dig into the ice, pushing the skater forward. This is like using resistance to turn current into useful voltage. When up to speed, the blades are turned to reduce friction, and the skater glides forward, conserving power by minimizing unwanted resistance.

100-watt resistor controls current in large power supplies

Inductor and transformer

AN INDUCTOR IS AN ELECTROMAGNET – a coil of wire, with or without a magnetic core, that produces magnetism when current flows through it. The magnetism forms a store of energy that takes time to fill or empty. Inductors, like capacitors (pp. 20-21), can introduce the time element into electronics. They can eliminate high-frequency currents, preventing voltage disturbances from getting into circuits or radio signals from getting out. With capacitors, they form electrical filters (pp. 34-35). Modern electronic technology uses inductors sparingly, because they are impossible to include in integrated circuits (pp. 52-53). A transformer is two or more coils sharing the same core. It is widely used to step voltages up or down. Changing current through one coil causes magnetic changes that affect all the coils, inducing the same voltage in each turn of wire. Coils with more turns have a higher induced voltage, but less current.

FARADAY'S RING
Michael Faraday discovered in 1831 that starting or stopping the current in one of the wires on this iron ring caused a brief rush of current in the other. The now famous ring is astonishingly like the modern transformer of 160 years later (opposite).

Terminal

Magnetron (p. 40) fits between these plates

Coils of wire

Magnetic core

MAGNETIC ENERGY
This electromagnet provided the magnetic field for an early magnetron (p. 40). The energy stored by this huge induction coil is demonstrated when it is switched off. The magnetic energy cannot disappear instantly, so neither can the current. The result is a fat spark at the switch as the magnet produces a high voltage that punches through air to keep the current going. It is like firing a cannon at a wall – the energy of the moving cannonball cannot disappear instantly, so it produces a force big enough to break bricks.

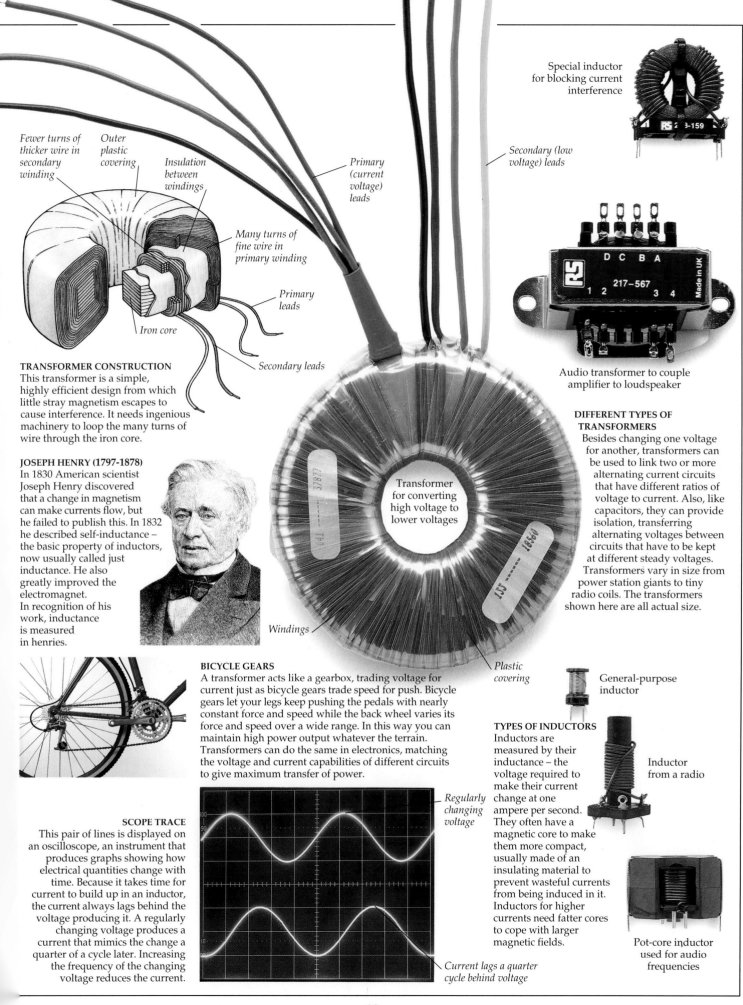

Special inductor for blocking current interference

Fewer turns of thicker wire in secondary winding

Outer plastic covering

Insulation between windings

Primary (current voltage) leads

Secondary (low voltage) leads

Many turns of fine wire in primary winding

Primary leads

Iron core

Secondary leads

TRANSFORMER CONSTRUCTION
This transformer is a simple, highly efficient design from which little stray magnetism escapes to cause interference. It needs ingenious machinery to loop the many turns of wire through the iron core.

JOSEPH HENRY (1797-1878)
In 1830 American scientist Joseph Henry discovered that a change in magnetism can make currents flow, but he failed to publish this. In 1832 he described self-inductance – the basic property of inductors, now usually called just inductance. He also greatly improved the electromagnet. In recognition of his work, inductance is measured in henries.

Windings

Transformer for converting high voltage to lower voltages

Plastic covering

Audio transformer to couple amplifier to loudspeaker

DIFFERENT TYPES OF TRANSFORMERS
Besides changing one voltage for another, transformers can be used to link two or more alternating current circuits that have different ratios of voltage to current. Also, like capacitors, they can provide isolation, transferring alternating voltages between circuits that have to be kept at different steady voltages. Transformers vary in size from power station giants to tiny radio coils. The transformers shown here are all actual size.

General-purpose inductor

Inductor from a radio

BICYCLE GEARS
A transformer acts like a gearbox, trading voltage for current just as bicycle gears trade speed for push. Bicycle gears let your legs keep pushing the pedals with nearly constant force and speed while the back wheel varies its force and speed over a wide range. In this way you can maintain high power output whatever the terrain. Transformers can do the same in electronics, matching the voltage and current capabilities of different circuits to give maximum transfer of power.

TYPES OF INDUCTORS
Inductors are measured by their inductance – the voltage required to make their current change at one ampere per second. They often have a magnetic core to make them more compact, usually made of an insulating material to prevent wasteful currents from being induced in it. Inductors for higher currents need fatter cores to cope with larger magnetic fields.

SCOPE TRACE
This pair of lines is displayed on an oscilloscope, an instrument that produces graphs showing how electrical quantities change with time. Because it takes time for current to build up in an inductor, the current always lags behind the voltage producing it. A regularly changing voltage produces a current that mimics the change a quarter of a cycle later. Increasing the frequency of the changing voltage reduces the current.

Regularly changing voltage

Current lags a quarter cycle behind voltage

Pot-core inductor used for audio frequencies

Capacitors

A CAPACITOR IS TWO OR MORE insulated metal plates, with every other plate connected to one of two wires. The insulation (the dielectric) prevents a current from flowing between the plates. Connect the capacitor to a battery, however, and current will flow briefly as electric charge builds up on the plates, stopping only when the increasing capacitor voltage equals the battery voltage. This process takes energy from the battery, which is stored in the dielectric. When used in electrical circuits, capacitors block direct currents but allow alternating currents to pass; this feature is exploited in electronics to isolate parts of a circuit that must be kept at different voltages while enabling signals to travel between them. Capacitors introduce time into electronics, allowing things to happen slowly or in sequence.

LEYDEN JAR

The capacitor is probably the oldest electronic component. In the 18th century, electricity was thought of as a fluid that passed through conductors and could be collected in jars like this. They are really capacitors, with metal coatings inside and outside acting as plates and the glass of the jar as the dielectric. The machine shown here produced a high voltage by rubbing a glass disk against cloth pads when the handle was turned. This could charge a nearby jar. In spite of the demise of the fluid theory, capacitors were still called condensers until about 1950.

BLOWING UP A BALLOON

You cannot blow through a balloon, but you can blow it up. As it fills, the pressure rises. Eventually, you cannot force in any more air or the balloon bursts. In the same way, current cannot flow through a capacitor but can flow into it. The voltage rises, stretching the molecules of the dielectric as electric charge builds up on the plates. The buildup stops when the battery is unable to force in any more charge or, if the voltage is too high, the overstretched dielectric gives way like the rubber of the balloon.

Voltage follows current

SCOPE TRACE

Because it takes time for charge to flow into a capacitor, its voltage always lags behind the current producing it. This oscilloscope trace shows how a regularly changing current produces a voltage that mimics the change a quarter of a cycle later. (On the oscilloscope screen, later times are shown toward the right-hand side.)

Regularly changing current

Metallized plastic plates

Outer plastic coating

End connector

Connecting wire

Capacitor for suppressing interference caused by electric motors

PME 271 Y
40/085/56

Metallized film capacitor with clear plastic coating

Miniature variable capacitor used for fine tuning inside radio and television sets

Construction of metallized film capacitor

DIFFERENT TYPES OF CAPACITORS

Every capacitor is a compromise between size, capacitance (ratio of charge to voltage), high-frequency performance, and maximum working voltage. The metallized film capacitor uses plastic coated with metal, like gift wrap. Many layers are sandwiched together, connected to wires, and dipped in plastic. Three types of capacitors are shown here actual size.

ELECTROLYTIC CAPACITOR
Large electrolytic capacitors like this one – shown here about two-thirds its actual size – are used to provide the reserve energy that smooths the current from a large power supply, perhaps in a mainframe computer. For a given volume and working voltage, electrolytic capacitors offer more capacitance than most other types.

Positive connection

Negative connection

Chemically impregnated paper

Aluminum foil

Aluminum can

Plastic insulation

SPACE SAVER
Capacitors with high capacitance can be large. One way to save space is with an electrolytic capacitor, which uses a chemical reaction to create dielectric layers only molecules thick. Because capacitance increases as dielectric thickness decreases, this kind of capacitor can pack a lot of energy into a small volume. The electrolytic capacitor is made by interleaving two strips of foil with paper soaked in a conducting solution, and rolling them up in a can. The dielectric is formed as a thin layer on the surface of one strip by a chemical reaction that takes place when a voltage is applied. If the capacitor is to keep working, this voltage must be maintained at all times.

ELECTRONIC WELCOME
A blizzard of electronically generated light greets the famous every year at the Cannes Film Festival in France. Before electronic flash, photographers used bulbs filled with magnesium wire. Each bulb gave only one flash and had to be changed before the next picture. But, like the electronic flash, the bulbs were often fired by discharging a capacitor.

FLASH CAMERA
A camera flash works by applying a short burst of high voltage to gas in a glass tube. The electrical energy required is small, but it has to be supplied quickly because the flash is so brief. A battery can neither supply the high voltage, nor deliver energy fast enough, so a capacitor is used instead. An electronic circuit steps up the battery voltage and charges the capacitor. When the button is pressed, the stored energy is released in about a thousandth of a second.

Flash head

Flash capacitor

Flexible printed circuit

Lens

Zoom control

See-through modern SLR camera with built-in zoom lens and electronic flash

Building circuits

ALL ELECTRONIC SYSTEMS are made from just a few basic components. By themselves, these components cannot do anything useful. It is the way they are connected to form circuits that creates the rich variety of electronic technology. Circuit design depends, among other things, on mathematics, much of it worked out in the 19th century. The rules governing the flow of electricity between components were formulated in 1845 by the German scientist Gustav Kirchhoff. Though simple, they are one of the keys to understanding how circuits work. For many basic functions, ready-made circuit designs exist in books, or can be pre-fabricated as integrated circuits (pp. 52-53). The designer has to know about these and decide how to link them to perform a given task. When the design is complete, the circuit must be built. Until the 1960s most circuits were put together by hand, with components linked by wires. The development of the printed circuit board – a piece of plastic with holes to accept the components and metal tracks to connect them – means that circuits can now be assembled by machine, greatly reducing the cost of electronic devices.

Series circuit

Battery

Positive connection goes to only one bulb

Negative connection goes to only one bulb

Dimly lit bulb

SERIES AND PARALLEL
The same components connected in different ways can behave quite differently. Connected in series, the battery voltage is split between these bulbs because they act as a voltage divider (pp. 16-17). The battery cannot drive much current through each bulb, and they light only dimly. Connected in parallel, each bulb has the whole of the battery voltage across it, so the battery can drive enough current through each bulb to give a bright light.

Battery

Parallel circuit

Positive and negative connections each go to both bulbs

Brightly lit bulb

Speaker

SARGROVE RADIO (1940S)
John Sargrove (1906-1974) was a British engineer who, in the 1940s, built machines that could make not just printed circuit boards, but complete radios like this one. His machines sprayed plastic blanks with metal to form circuits including resistors, inductors, and capacitors. They even attached large components like electron tube holders. Only electron tube insertion and final adjustment needed human hands. His ideas were sound, but his machines were thought to threaten jobs.

Tuning capacitor

Tuning knob

Vacuum tube

Front view of radio

Capacitor

Inductor

Plastic plate

Side view of Sargrove radio

CIRCUIT LAWS
The German physicist Gustav Kirchhoff (1824-1887) extended Ohm's law (pp. 16-17) to deal with situations where more than one resistor was connected to more than one battery. His circuit laws state that all the current flowing into any point must also flow out of it, and that the total voltage driving current around any loop must equal the total of the voltages opposing it. These simple principles allow complicated circuits to be analyzed mathematically. They are used by computer programs that help in circuit design.

AC CIRCUIT

Most electronic circuits carry voltages and currents that continually reverse their direction. They are called alternating current (AC) circuits. Inductors and capacitors respond to AC in different ways. At low frequencies, the inductor offers little opposition to the current, so only a small voltage appears across it, while the capacitor opposes the current more strongly, producing a higher voltage. The situation is reversed at high frequencies. The voltages across inductor and capacitor are in opposite directions. At just one frequency – the resonant frequency – they will cancel out, allowing large currents to flow. This effect is used in filters (pp. 34-35).

Signal generator produces signals ranging from low to high frequency

Capacitor produces large voltage *Inductor produces small voltage* *Inductor produces large voltage* *Capacitor produces small voltage*

Inductor

Low frequency   High frequency

Meter measuring total current in milliamperes (mA)

280 mA

Current splits here into 90 and 190 mA

Currents flowing out add up to 280 mA

Capacitor

90 mA

190 mA

2.0 V

Battery terminal

Voltages across R1 and R4 add up to 9 volts

R1

2.8 V

Meter

9.0 V

R2

R3

R4

6.2 V

Voltages across R1, R2, and R3 add up to 9 volts

4.2 V

Battery

PAUL EISLER (1907-1992)

Until German engineer Paul Eisler perfected the printed circuit board, electronic equipment was built laboriously by hand. Eisler used printing methods to etch away thin copper foil stuck to plastic sheets. The first printed circuit boards were fitted inside anti-aircraft shells in the 1940s.

Paul Eisler

DC CIRCUIT

This is a direct current (DC) circuit because the currents flow steadily in one direction. The meters show how Kirchhoff's circuit laws function. The currents flowing out of any point add up to the current flowing in. The voltages around any path between the battery terminals add up to the battery voltage. The actual voltages and currents depend on the resistor values and are given by Ohm's law.

Tracks connecting components

PRINTED CIRCUIT BOARD

Printed circuit boards, like this one from a small computer, are made from plastic coated with copper foil. The foil is etched away to leave tracks that connect the components together. A layer of lacquer protects the board except where components are inserted. This allows the components to be fixed in place by skimming the entire board across a bath of molten solder. More elaborate boards have several layers of tracks.

THE LANGUAGE OF ELECTRONICS

Electronics engineers use special units to measure both electricity and the properties of components. They also use a visual language in which every component has a standard symbol. These symbols can be linked to form diagrams showing exactly how a circuit is made.

BASIC UNITS

A = ampere (unit of current)

V = volt (unit of voltage)

W = watt (unit of power)

Ω = ohm (unit of resistance)

H = henry (unit of inductance)

F = farad (unit of capacitance)

Hz = hertz (unit of frequency)

PREFIXES TO INDICATE FRACTIONS OR MULTIPLES OF UNITS

p = pico (1 trillionth)

n = nano (1 billionth)

μ = micro (1 millionth)

m = milli (1 thousandth)

k = kilo (1 thousand)

M = mega (1 million)

G = giga (1 billion)

CIRCUIT SYMBOLS

battery

resistor

potentiometer

inductor

transformer

capacitor

pre-set capacitor

electrolytic capacitor

diode

light-emitting diode

bipolar transistor

field effect transistor

Communicating with electricity

THE DISCOVERIES OF OERSTED and Faraday (pp. 10-11) led to significant changes in people's lives. A telegraph message traveled 100 million times faster than a horse or ship, enabling nations to trade efficiently over vast areas of the globe. Electric light was brighter and cheaper than gas, extending the day for work and leisure. But the biggest effect was to give people the power of information. Railroads used the telegraph to aid their operations and to distribute newspapers carrying reports telegraphed from all over the world. Some of the effects of electrical science seemed magical. The theoretical work of British mathematician James Clerk Maxwell (1831-1879) and German physicist Heinrich Hertz (1857-1894) led, by 1900, to communication with ships on the high seas. All of this was accomplished with only the crudest means of amplifying and detecting the faltering signals that crossed oceans and continents.

SIMPLE COMMUNICATION
The first electric telegraphs all used more than one wire. It was American portrait painter Samuel F. B. Morse (1791-1872) who realized that, given a suitable code tapped out by a key, a single wire could carry any message.

Receiving dial

Transmitting dial   *Handle turns generator inside*   *Terminal*

Transmit/receive switch

Letter button

SIEMENS GALVANOMETER
Rain and storm damage caused electricity to leak from telegraph wires and produce bad contacts. Galvanometers like this one, made in about 1890, were used to find faults by comparing the currents in two similar wires. A large difference indicated a problem. Inside the apparatus a magnetized needle is suspended over a pair of coils – one coil for each wire. The terminals are connected to the telegraph wires being tested.

Magnetized needle

Terminal

TELEGRAPHY ON THE BATTLEFIELD
In 1864, near the end of the American Civil War, Ulysses S. Grant (1822-1885) took command of the Union armies. By using the telegraph to keep in contact with his far-flung troops, he defeated the Confederate forces. Grant realized that the telegraph could provide him with vital information.

PORTABLE ABC TELEGRAPH
British musical instrument maker and professor of experimental philosophy Sir Charles Wheatstone (1802-1875) always tried hard to make his electric telegraphs as easy to use as possible. This ABC telegraph of 1858 was so simple that an operator could use it after a few minutes training. To transmit a message, the handle was turned and the buttons pressed. A generator inside created electrical impulses that made a similar needle at the receiving end rotate in step, pausing at the letters of the message.

BUSINESS VENTURES
The telephone made business communications between companies in different countries much quicker. The first telephone link between London and Paris was opened with much ceremony in 1891.

EDISON TELEPHONE
This strange-looking telephone was designed by Thomas Edison (1847-1931) because he needed to avoid using the transmitter and receiver already patented by Bell in 1876. Edison's transmitter was effective, but his receiver was too inconvenient to survive.

Bell to signal incoming call

Drum inside receiver is sensitive to incoming currents

Handle turns drum

Transmitter uses varying resistance of carbon to send speech

ALEXANDER GRAHAM BELL
Bell (1847-1922) was a Scot who taught the deaf in America. In 1876 he devised the first successful telephone, using magnetism and electricity to produce a simple, reliable system. The telephone was the first really easy-to-use device for communicating at a distance.

Battery supplies current to operate the relay

Relay links the signal and the circuit

Antenna transformer to increase efficiency

Coherer

Tapper restores coherer to non-conducting state

MARCONI RECEIVER
This 1899 receiver by Italian inventor Guglielmo Marconi (1874-1937) detects messages sent as bursts of radio waves. With this equipment, the messages can be treated as if they had come by wire. The vital component is the coherer – a device that conducts electricity only when subjected to radio waves. The receiver uses an electromagnetic relay to convert the small coherer current into a large telegraph current.

Transmitter varies current as pencil moves

Clockwork to drive rollers

Rollers

COWPER'S WRITING TELEGRAPH
Telegraph comes from two Greek words meaning "writing at a distance." In 1878 British engineer William Cowper (1819-1893) took this literally and designed a machine that could reproduce a message being written by someone many miles away. Although working on a completely different principle, it was a distant (and unsuccessful) cousin of today's fax machine (pp. 60-61).

Paper tape

Rollers pull tape through machine

Handwritten message reproduced at distant receiver

Pencil connected to motion transmitters

Moving electrons

Everything around us is made of atoms. Atoms themselves are made of still smaller particles called protons, neutrons, and electrons. Electrons are the tiniest of these particles. Each one of them carries the smallest possible amount of negative electricity, and even tiny bits of matter contain billions of electrons. In most materials, and especially in good insulators like glass or plastics, electrons are held firmly in place by the heavier, positively charged protons. But some materials, mostly metals, contain electrons that are more mobile. This allows such materials to be used for conducting electricity from one place to another and means that metals are good conductors. They are used for this purpose in all electrical systems. When metals are heated, their electrons are given still more energy, sometimes enough to break free completely, like rockets escaping the pull of the Earth.

NAMING THE ELECTRON
In 1897 the British physicist J. J. Thomson (1856-1940) found that he could use many different materials to obtain negatively charged particles with exactly the same properties. He called these particles electrons. For his experiments he used a glass tube with metal plates inside it and with most of the air pumped out. It was called a cathode ray tube and had been developed by scientists investigating the effect of electricity on gases.

Electrons holding metal together

Mobile electron

Proton

Cool metal

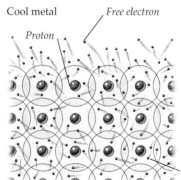

Free electron

Proton

Mobile electron

Heated metal

Electron

The electron takes a helical track

Direction of magnetic field

ELECTRON STRUCTURE OF METALS
Although metals contain plenty of mobile electrons, few of the electrons have enough energy at normal temperatures to break free from the atomic force that holds them inside the material. Heating metals up to quite modest temperatures – cooler than the filament of a light bulb – makes a big difference to the energy of their electrons, allowing many of them to escape into space. Once free, preferably in a vacuum where there is nothing to bump into, they can be guided by electricity or magnetism to form a controlled electric current. This is the basic principle of the vacuum tube (pp. 28-29), which was once the backbone of electronics, and the cathode ray tube, which is still the best way of showing television pictures.

ELECTRONIC CHARGE
Robert Millikan (1868-1953) was an American physicist who deduced the actual charge of the electron in 1911. He did this by measuring the electric charge of an oil droplet.

THE PATH OF A MOVING ELECTRON
A moving electron constitutes an electric current and so creates a magnetic field (pp. 10-11). Another magnetic field can interact with this, producing a path that varies from a tight coil, used in a magnetron (p. 40), to a straight line, used in a high-power klystron (p. 41).

Vacuum

Picture amplifier

HEAD AMPLIFIER A 12

AURORA BOREALIS
These spectacular night-sky displays are seen near the Earth's poles. They happen when electrons and protons, ejected by the Sun, hit the upper atmosphere and are trapped in the Earth's magnetic field.

Image plate covered with tiny globules of light-sensitive metal

EARLY TELEVISION
A television camera scans the picture from its lens, turning it into a stream of information that can be sent down a cable. To get realistic detail and movement, this has to be done quickly. In the 1930s, when television was being developed, only a beam of electrons could move fast enough.

Lens

Deflection coils

MAKING PICTURES
In this Emitron television camera, the beam of electrons used to scan the picture was generated by a gun at the end of the sloping tube and swept across the image plate by magnetic fields. (Brief exposure to a magnetic field will deflect electrons from one straight path to another. If the field is changed in the right pattern, an electron beam can be made to scan a rectangular area). The image plate was covered with thousands of tiny globules of an alloy of silver and cesium. Separated from a metal back plate by a thin layer of insulation, these formed photosensitive capacitors (pp. 20-21) that charged up in the light of the image. As the electron beam touched each capacitor, completing a circuit, it discharged, sending current to an amplifier (pp. 30-31). More current flowed where the picture was brighter.

Vacuum tube

Electron gun

EXPERIMENTING WITH ELECTRONS
Wilhelm Röntgen (1845-1923), a German physicist and the first winner of the Nobel Prize for physics, was experimenting with cathode rays in 1895 when he noticed that his tubes could make a screen glow – even when there was something in the way. He had discovered X-rays. They are emitted whenever fast-moving electrons are stopped in their tracks. The tubes he used were, like Thomson's, made of glass and fitted with metal plates called electrodes. Inside was a partial vacuum.
When high voltage was applied, electrons were torn from the negative electrode (cathode) by the attraction of the positive electrode (anode). They could make the glass or special screens glow. If the voltage was high enough, the electrons could create X-rays when they hit the anode. Later X-ray tubes, like the one shown, use a heated cathode.

End cap connects to electricity supply

Heated cathode emits electrons

Tungsten anode emits X-rays when electrons hit it

Glass envelope

Vacuum

Using electrons

IT TOOK EXPERIMENTERS NEARLY 30 YEARS to realize that electrons given off by hot metals could be used to amplify signals. Thomas Edison suspected as early as 1880 that something was traveling through the vacuum inside his light bulbs. In 1904 Ambrose Fleming used this Edison effect to make a device that he called a valve because it conducted electricity one way only. This diode – it has two electrodes – could detect weak radio waves by turning their alternating current into direct current (p. 23) that worked an indicator, but could not increase their power. When Lee De Forest added a third electrode, creating the triode, it became possible to convert a weak signal into a strong one, making the first true amplifier.

Wire to plate

Wire to grid

Plate

Grid

MINIATURE DIODE
Small glass-based diodes like this appeared in the 1940s. They were the most common type in use when diodes began to be replaced by transistors in the late 1950s (pp. 38-39).

FLEMING EXPERIMENTAL BULB
John Ambrose Fleming (1849-1945), a British professor of electrical engineering, investigated Edison's light bulbs in 1889 (see below). He used bulbs like this with an extra wire electrode inside. Fleming remembered them in 1904 while seeking a detector for radio waves. He realized that electrons from the filament could only flow one way, because they would be repelled if the wire became more negative than the filament. This led to his oscillation vacuum tube, which acted on the oscillating radio currents like the one-way valve of a tire, turning them into steady current to work a telegraph.

Vacuum

Glass bulb

Vacuum

Glass bulb

Filament

Carbon filament

Connection to anode

Anode

Wooden base

AUDION TRIODE
Invented by Lee De Forest in 1906, this Audion triode of 1907 was adapted from a car headlamp bulb. The crucial difference from Fleming's earlier vacuum tubes was an extra wire or grid positioned in the path of the electrons. This could control them, making amplification possible. With three electrodes (filament, grid, and plate), the Audion is a triode. Its primitive design meant that it hardly amplified at all, but it was a sensitive radio detector.

Negative filament connection through retaining screw

Positive filament connection through end contact

ELECTRONS IN LIGHT BULBS
Thomas Alva Edison (1847-1931) was one of America's most famous inventors. While solving the problem of electric lighting, he accidentally sowed the seed of electronics. Trying to understand why the glass of his light bulbs went dark with age, he realized that something was traveling from the negative to the positive side of the filaments.

Wire to anode

Wire to filament

VALVE IN A PIPELINE
Vacuum tubes work rather like a valve in an oil pipe. Pressure in the pipe forces the oil one way. By adjusting the position of a gate inside the pipe, as here on a Libyan desert pipeline, the flow can be controlled. In a similar way, electrons attracted from negative cathode to positive anode are controlled by the varying negative voltage of the grid in between.

HOW A TRIODE WORKS

A triode is a valve with three electrodes (wires or plates) inside it. A heated electrode, the cathode, emits electrons. They are attracted to the anode, which is at a more positive voltage than the cathode, but are slowed down by the grid, which carries the varying voltage to be amplified. This makes the electron current vary. The varying current is made to flow through a resistor (pp. 16-17), which converts it into a magnified copy of the input voltage.

Anode resistor

Anode

Output voltage

Electrons

Grid

Cathode

Input voltage

Heater

LEE DE FOREST (1873-1961)
De Forest was the American physicist who made the first electronic amplifier – the triode. In 1906, he added a wire grid to the hardware that was accumulating in the simple light bulb to make the first triode.

LARGE TRANSMITTING TRIODE
Vacuum tubes use moving electrons liberated by heat (pp. 26-27), so are called thermionic, from the Greek words meaning heat and going. The electrons are controlled by plates or wires called electrodes. This high-power vacuum, tube with three electrodes is a triode. The electrode that attracts the electrons becomes very hot, so it is made of carbon to stop it from melting.

Top cap connecting to anode

Glass envelope

Carbon anode

A.E.I.
14D14
MADE IN ENGLAND

Silver coating mops up last traces of air to create vacuum

Triode

Terminal to connect to loudspeaker

Vacuum

Pins connecting to other electrodes

STERLING AMPLIFIER
By the 1920s triodes were effective amplifiers and could be used in the home to drive loudspeakers. But they were extremely expensive and low powered. This 1925 amplifier gave out about as much power as a modern transistor radio.

Amplifiers

AMPLIFIERS TURN WEAK ELECTRICAL SIGNALS into stronger ones. They allow a small amount of power, representing information, to control a much larger amount of power that can do useful work. In this way amplifiers make the vital link between information and energy. Making vacuum tubes or transistors amplify requires care if their output is not to be a distorted version of their input. In 1927, Harold Black solved this problem with his idea of negative feedback – an amplifier monitors and corrects its own errors. Feedback of another kind can turn an amplifier into an oscillator (p. 33). Further, an amplifier driven hard enough, so that its output is forced to one extreme or the other, can act as an electrically controlled switch. Computers contain huge assemblies of such switches. In these machines, information controls not just energy but more information, demonstrating the might of the amplifier.

USING A MEGAPHONE ON THE FILM SET
An amplifier is not just anything that makes things bigger or louder. A true amplifier turns raw power into controlled power. The megaphone makes sounds louder but is not an amplifier, because all it does is use the existing power of the voice more efficiently.

A HOMELY AMP
An amplifier is essential for family listening. Without one, headphones must be used, as radio circuits do not give enough power to work a loudspeaker. The low-powered amplifier in this 1940s radio entertained the children without annoying the neighbors.

BROWN REPEATER
Amplifying a continuously varying signal like a telephone call was difficult without electronics, but not impossible. The Brown repeater of 1918 was installed at telephone exchanges to boost long-distance calls. It exploited the amplifying ability of the carbon granule microphone also used in telephones (p. 25). It contained one of these microphones pressed against an iron reed that reproduced the sound of the call to be amplified. It produced severe distortion.

Terminal

Coils to energize magnet

Coils for incoming telephone currents

Delicate steel reed vibrates in magnetic field

Capsule of carbon changes resistance when vibrated

AUDIO AMPLIFIER
Early radios produced little power, so extra amplifiers were often added. There was no industry producing them on a large scale, but they could always be built at home, like this magnificent creation of the late 1920s. Big amplifiers need plenty of raw power to work, and this one had a hefty power supply. It also used two vacuum tubes to drive the loudspeaker (pp. 42-43), one pushing, the other pulling. A similar arrangement is still used in modern amplifiers.

Radio signal input 0.000000001 W

Intermediate output 0.01 W

Heat 2 W *Heat 2 W*

Audio output 2 W *Heat 1.95 W*

Intermediate frequency amplifier 2 W

Audio amplifier 4 W

Power supply

Actual sound output 0.05 W

Loudspeaker

Power input 8 W

Heat 2 W

RADIO POWER FLOWS
A radio uses a chain of amplifiers to feed power from the wall socket, under the control of an incredibly small amount of power from the antenna, to the speaker. Nearly all of it is wasted as heat by the time it reaches the speaker, but because ears are very sensitive it still sounds loud.

Capacitor
smooths
supply
voltage

Low
power
valve
tube

Transformer
changes voltage to
suit amplifier

Large inductor

Variable
resistor

High-power
vacuum tubes
drive loudspeaker

Rectifier diode
converts AC
household power
to DC for
vacuum tubes

HAROLD S. BLACK (1898-1983)
In 1927, Harold S. Black was working at the
Bell Telephone Laboratories in America trying
to design amplifiers that would not distort
signals. He realized that subtracting a little of
an amplifier's output from its input, while
reducing its amplification, would also reduce the
distortion. Simple mathematics proved that this
negative feedback could make a bad amplifier
into a good one. It has been used ever since.

Output
transformer
delivers
power in
form
suited to
loudspeaker

Power relay

Operational
amplifier

Audio amplifier

**AMPLIFYING
COMPONENTS**
Although not a true
amplifier, the relay can be
used to switch heavy
currents or, in a smaller
version, to connect and
disconnect signals.
Amplifiers available as
integrated circuits
(pp. 52-53) can perform
many functions. The
audio amplifier can
deliver more than 20
watts to a suitable
speaker. Operational
amplifiers have a
wide range of uses
in low-power
analog circuits.
The components
above are shown
actual size.

Volume control

31

Oscillators

Gold electrode

Quartz crystal

Envelope

QUARTZ CRYSTAL
Quartz crystals are used where accurate, constant frequency really matters. They are piezoelectric – a voltage makes them bend or stretch, while bending or stretching them produces a voltage. An amplifier, its input coming from the vibrating crystal itself, can keep the thin slice of quartz (this one is sealed in an evacuated glass envelope) oscillating mechanically at up to 10 million times per second.

Fingerboard

Adjustable pickup

Adjustable pickup

Volume and tone controls

Output connection to amplifier

WHEELS, ENDLESSLY REPEATING THE SAME MOTION, provide power, movement, or timing for machines. Oscillators do the same in electronics, producing continually repeated patterns of voltage or current that can move an electron beam, supply pulses to control a computer, or generate waves that carry signals through cables or space. An oscillator can be made by connecting the output of an amplifier to its own input through something that delays the signal. If the delay is arranged so that at just one frequency the rising and falling voltages at the input and output of the amplifier stay in step, they will reinforce each other and build up into a continually repeating pattern. Only a little power is needed to keep this pattern going. The amplifier can deliver the rest to do useful work in other circuits.

Frets control vibrating length of string, fixing frequency

Vibrating steel string

Permanent magnet

Coil

Magnetic pickup

PRODUCING NOTES
Every oscillator contains three basic elements – something that fixes the frequency, an amplifier, and a feedback path. An electric guitar, together with its amp and speaker, provides all of these and can behave like an oscillator. True oscillators produce waves that continue indefinitely, while the guitar, because the feedback path is imperfect, cannot quite achieve this. Plucking a guitar string causes vibration at a definite frequency. This normally fades away quite quickly. With a magnetic pickup in place, the steel string, vibrating near the magnet, creates a voltage in a coil that can be sent to an amplifier. This not only makes the sound louder, it can also make it last longer, by feeding back power in the form of sound from a speaker.

Input connection from guitar

Speaker

Amplifier

Types of oscillators

There are two basic kinds of oscillators. Both need amplifiers, but the frequency is fixed in different ways. Relaxation oscillators accumulate energy until it causes a switch (a kind of amplifier) to operate, dumping the energy and starting the cycle again. Their frequency is not very constant. Harmonic oscillators accumulate energy in one form at the expense of another, then swap it back. An amplifier replaces any energy lost. Although it produces waves of only one shape, this kind of oscillator is accurate and widely used in electronics.

WATER SCARECROW IN THE GARDEN
Water at a height stores energy. As the bucket of this mechanical relaxation oscillator fills, it gets heavier and overbalances, dumping its energy with the water (and scaring any stray animals in the garden). It can then swing back and fill again. The frequency is fixed by the time this takes. An electronic equivalent is a capacitor slowly charging until it operates a switch that quickly discharges it.

Balance wheel

Escapement wheel

Hairspring

CLOCK ESCAPEMENT
This mechanical harmonic oscillator – the escapement mechanism in a clock – stores energy as motion of the wheel and as strain in the spring. Energy swaps between the two as the wheel speeds and slows and the spring coils and uncoils. The escapement acts as an amplifier, feeding in energy from the clock. The frequency is fixed by the stiffness of the spring and the mass and shape of the wheel. The electronic equivalent is a capacitor and inductor connected together, swapping electric and magnetic energy in a similar way to produce high-frequency oscillations.

Cathode ray tube

Position control

Brightness control

Control for internal sweep oscillator frequency

Synchronization control gives steady picture

Width control

Height control

OSCILLOSCOPE
Seeing the waves made by oscillators was difficult until German scientist Ferdinand Braun (1850-1918) invented a form of cathode ray oscilloscope in 1897. This one was made around 1945. An internal oscillator repeatedly sweeps a beam of electrons across the screen at constant speed. The input voltage moves the beam up and down, drawing a picture of the wave. Modern oscilloscopes often display the picture digitally, sometimes on a computer screen (pp. 56-57).

ANIMAL TRACKER
Scientists can study the behavior of penguins in the Antarctic by fitting them with a radio tracking device. This is a combined harmonic and relaxation oscillator that transmits in short bursts, saving the battery. Using a directional antenna, researchers can follow the beeps and map the birds' movements.

How filters work

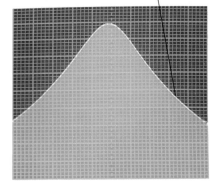

SIEVING ACCORDING TO SIZE
A sieve is similar to a low-pass filter in electronics. It allows everything below a certain size to get through. What is left behind in the sieve has been high-pass filtered – it consists of everything above a certain size.

FILTERS, IN COFFEEMAKERS, ETC., are familiar in everyday life. In electronics, filters almost always respond to the frequency of signals (pp. 14-15) – passing low, high, or a chosen band of frequencies – and blocking others. Filters are needed because real signals contain a mixture of frequencies, not all of them useful. A radio antenna, for example, picks up a multitude of stations, but a filter ensures that only one gets through at a time. Other filters block everything above a given frequency, maybe to reduce hiss on old tapes. Low frequencies can be blocked too, perhaps to remove the rumble produced by an old record player. Filters can use either analog or digital techniques (pp. 46-47). Analog filters have been used since the 19th century. They rely on the way inductors and capacitors respond to different frequencies. Digital filters use fast microprocessors (pp. 58-59) to transform the signal mathematically into one without the unwanted frequencies.

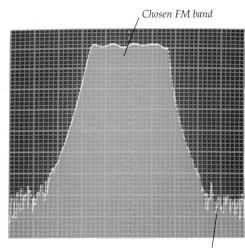

FUEL GAUGE
The fuel gauge in a car responds to the level of liquid in the tank. The level varies wildly as the car goes over bumps, but the reading remains steady because it is low-pass filtered to remove rapid changes. This can be seen when the car is first switched on – the fuel reading takes several seconds to reach its true value.

Filter response has wide skirts that let unwanted signals through

INEFFICIENT BAND-PASS FILTER
Band-pass filters block both low and high frequencies and allow through a chosen band only. This trace shows how a poor-quality filter, using an inductor that absorbs signal energy, can produce wide skirts that let unwanted signals through, as well as the chosen band.

Tuning knob

Variable capacitor

EARLY RADIO-TUNED CIRCUIT (*left*)
Until the 1980s, rejection of unwanted radio stations was partly done by components like this. A fixed inductor is used with a variable capacitor – connected to the tuning knob – to form a variable band-pass filter that can be tuned to the frequency of the wanted station. In this homemade receiver of the late 1920s the signal passes through several such filters, each of which has to be separately tuned by hand.

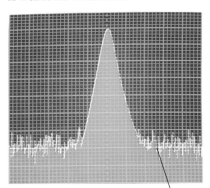

NARROW FILTER
Careful design of a simple band-pass filter, using an inductor and a capacitor resonating at the center of the band, can give good rejection of unwanted frequencies. But the shape of the filter's response means that some wanted frequencies will be rejected too.

Unwanted frequencies reduced

Fixed inductor

Vacuum tube

Chosen FM band

FM FILTER
Simple filters are not good enough for an FM radio signal, with its very wide spectrum (p. 49). Filters using several resonators tuned to different frequencies can produce a response that, as this spectrum-analyzer image shows, is reasonably flat while giving good rejection outside the wanted band. The resonators are often quartz crystals or ceramic plates.

Rejected frequencies

MECHANICAL FILTER

Some types of filters can absorb most of the signal's unwanted energy. The springs and shock absorbers in the forks of this bike form a mechanical low-pass filter that transforms destructive energy, released as the bike hits the ground, into harmless heat. The filter partially isolates the rider from the vertical motion of the wheels, making the ride just a little less uncomfortable.

Absorbent plastic prevents waves reflecting back

Comb of electrodes makes quartz ripple at one wavelength

Metal package

Quartz plate

Connecting wire

A COMPONENT FOR RADAR AND TELEVISION

The properties of traveling waves (pp. 12-13) can be used in filters. Structures in their path can block some wavelengths while helping others on their way. Electromagnetic waves travel so fast that these structures might need to be very large. By converting the waves to much slower ripples on the surface of a quartz plate, compact and effective surface acoustic wave (SAW) filters for radar and television can be made.

HIGH- AND LOW-PASS FILTERS

Filters are never perfect. These two displays show that instead of unwanted frequencies being completely blocked, a little of their power creeps through. As with all filters, there is also a region where signals are neither totally blocked nor totally passed. (On the spectrum-analyzer screen, higher frequencies are shown towards the right-hand side.)

Cut-off frequency

Cut-off frequency

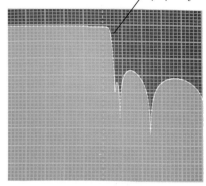

A high-pass filter lets through frequencies above its cut-off frequency

A low-pass filter mirrors the high-pass filter, letting through only low frequencies

TUNING A RADIO

Modern radios use a variable filter followed by a fixed-frequency filter. To select a particular station, its frequency is changed to the filter's fixed frequency by mixing the signal with one generated by a variable-frequency oscillator (pp. 32-33). When the tuning knob is turned, the variable filter tunes to the wanted station, while the oscillator adjusts its frequency to shift the station into the band passed by the fixed filter.

Magic eye shows maximum light when tuning is correct

Tuning scale indicates frequency

FM selector button

Tuning knob

Semiconductors

SEMICONDUCTORS ARE THE KEY to modern electronics. These materials are electrical conductors that are nearly insulators. Unlike metals, only a few of their electrons roam free, while others hop from atom to atom, leaving holes which act like positive charges moving the opposite way. Adding impurities to semiconductors, a process called doping, changes the way they conduct, allowing solid structures to be created in which electrons can be controlled electrically. Silicon is a semiconductor that has been used in components since the earliest days of radio. It is now the mainstay of electronics. In the early 1940s, however, it was the rare element germanium that seemed more promising for better radar detectors. By 1945 it was being used in attempts to make a semiconductor device that would amplify (pp. 38-39).

CRYSTAL SET
The crystal radio set, popular in the 1920s, was called after the semiconductor crystal that it used. By twiddling a fine wire – the cat's whisker – you could find a spot on the crystal where a one-way current would pass, allowing the sound signal carried by the radio waves to operate the headphones. In the 1940s scientists started trying to understand how devices like this, developed by trial and error, really worked. This eventually led to a huge expansion of the semiconductor industry.

End where crystal was pulled from vat of molten silicon

Each square is a silicon chip

Test pattern

Diamond-tipped saw separates chips along cutting line

SILICON WAFER
Slicing and polishing a large semiconductor crystal yields thin disks or wafers on which microscopic electronic components can be created by selective doping, forming integrated circuits (pp. 52-53). Silicon is preferred because it is cheap and strong.

SILICON CRYSTAL
Silicon is by far the most widely used semiconductor. Like its earlier rival germanium, silicon atoms have four outer electrons, but unlike germanium, silicon is not rare. After oxygen it is the second most abundant element on Earth. Its electrons are less mobile than those of germanium, but it is also less temperature sensitive. Large crystals like this are formed by pulling them slowly out of a vat of molten material.

Silicon

Gold mount

SILICON LOCKET
The properties of silicon have been known for nearly a century. This chunk was originally part of a radio detector, but is now mounted as a piece of jewelry. It was used in 1910 on the first British cargo ship to carry radio, the SS *Nonsuch*.

Body of crystal

A BOUNTEOUS MATERIAL
The starting point for microchips is sand, a compound of silicon and oxygen. By melting sand with other materials, the silicon can be extracted, but making a crystal good enough for chips needs repeated refining until impurities are down to less than one atom in a billion.

SEMICONDUCTOR ELEMENTS

When the Russian chemist Dmitri Mendeleyev (1834-1907) listed the elements in order of atomic weight, he found that elements with similar properties appeared at regular intervals. He constructed a table in which related elements appear in vertical groups. Gaps in this table allowed him to predict properties of undiscovered elements. One, in a gap below silicon, he called ekasilicon. This semiconductor was found in 1886 by the German chemist Clemens Winkler (1838-1904). He named it germanium, after his country.

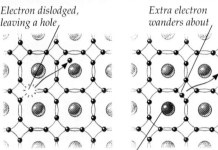

Semiconductors

Cathode lead

THE PERIODIC TABLE

Most of the elements in the periodic table are metals. About 20 on the right of the table are nonmetals. The semiconducting elements lie between. Some are only semiconducting in a particular state. Many semiconducting compounds that are made up of more than one semiconducting element.

DOPING SEMICONDUCTORS

Intrinsic silicon conducts slightly because a few electrons have enough energy to escape from their atoms. Others hop into the resulting holes, leaving new holes behind. The electrons and the moving holes each carry half the current. Adding a proportion of atoms with five outer electrons increases the number of electrons and reduces the number of holes, giving n-type silicon, a better conductor in which electrons carry most of the current. Adding atoms with only three outer electrons reduces the number of electrons, but increases the number of holes, forming p-type silicon in which holes carry most of the current.

Electron dislodged, leaving a hole

Extra electron wanders about

Atom is an electron short

Hole moves

Intrinsic semiconductor

Impurity atom

n-type semiconductor

p-type semiconductor

Cooling fin

Nut maintains pressure between plates

Oxidized copper plate

SMALL AND QUICK

This tiny silicon diode is useful for controlling signals. Its small size means that it can work at high frequencies.

SILICON DIODE

A silicon crystal with adjoining p- and n-type regions forms a diode, a device that conducts electricity in one direction only. Holes leak out of the p-type region into the n-type region, and electrons do the opposite. This creates an electrical imbalance that eventually stops the electrons from moving. Applying a voltage one way makes the imbalance worse, so no current flows. A small voltage the other way overcomes the imbalance and allows current through. The large diode here (both diodes are shown actual size) is used for big power supplies. It will withstand 400 volts in the wrong direction and handle a current of 240 amps.

Tiny diode

Anode stud

Large diode

Connecting tag

METAL RECTIFIER

Semiconductors were in use throughout much of the thermionic valve (diode) era (pp. 28-29). Copper in contact with copper oxide, a semiconductor, conducts electricity much better in one direction than the other, forming a diode. Stacks of oxidized copper plates were used to rectify the alternating voltage of household electricity, creating the steady voltage needed by radio tubes. The cat's whisker detector used in crystal sets also depended on a contact between metal and semiconductor to form a rectifying diode.

CARBORUNDUM

When chemically combined with its close relation carbon, silicon forms a hard, often iridescent, semiconducting material called silicon carbide, or Carborundum. It was widely used in early radio detectors, but is now employed only as an abrasive.

Development of the transistor

IN 1947, INCREASED UNDERSTANDING of the physics of solids led to the creation of the transistor, a semiconductor amplifier that has had an impact out of all proportion to its size. The earliest semiconductor devices were diodes (p. 37) that, with their one-way conduction, are still useful for turning alternating into direct current (pp. 22-23). But the transistor could replace a key electronic component, the triode (p. 37), duplicating its ability to amplify and switch without the need for a large, fragile glass envelope or power-hungry heater. The transistor was originally conceived as a possible replacement for electromechanical switches in telephone exchanges. Forty years of development have changed it into a microscopic pattern etched into the surface of a slice of silicon (pp. 52-53). Many devices we now take for granted would be unrecognizable without the transistor. A VCR would need at least eight times the space, a personal computer would fill a room, and both would be fantastically expensive.

THE MAN IN THE STREET
The transistor lit the fuse to an information explosion that continues today. By the late 1950s this man, who was probably born before the development of modern electronics, had instant access to news, even standing in the street. Today personal radios and cassette machines are seen in public places everywhere.

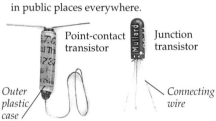

Point-contact transistor

Junction transistor

Outer plastic case

Connecting wire

DIFFERENT TYPES OF TRANSISTORS
The transistor has evolved into many different types and adapted to different jobs. Those shown here are actual size. Some are good at amplifying small radio frequency signals. Others are slower but can handle large currents and voltages. There are also devices related to the transistor that behave quite differently. The thyristor, once triggered into conducting electricity, stays switched on without further input, just like a mechanical switch.

Thyristor used in lamp dimmers

Transistor for high-frequency analog circuits

Power transistor in plastic pack

Transistor for controlling electric motors

EARLY TRANSISTORS
William Shockley (1910-1989), leader of the team that invented the point-contact transistor, went on to invent the more reliable junction type. Point-contact transistors, based directly on the original invention of 1947, were produced commercially until the early 1950s. Two contact wires and a base connection were positioned on a germanium crystal, which was then sealed into a can. These devices were highly unreliable and added a lot of noise to signals. In the junction transistor, the wire probes are replaced by blobs of p-type germanium fused to an n-type base (p.37). These components were the first practical commercial transistors and were used from about 1950 to 1955.

Supporting frame

Spring pushes probes onto crystal

Emitter connection

Collector connection

Germanium crystal

Base connection

THE FIRST TRANSISTOR
This replica of the first working transistor, which is about 4 in (10 cm) high, resembles the cat's whisker detector of early radio sets, but it is a semiconductor amplifier. Two pointed wires probe the surface of a germanium crystal, while a third connection is made to the base. A change in current through one probe causes a larger change in current through the other.

Block holding two wire probes

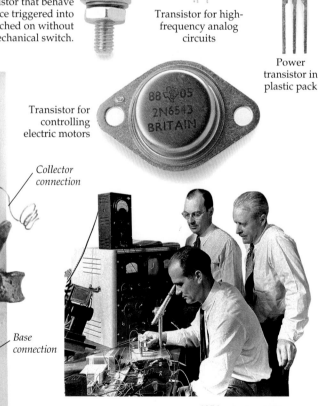

1956 NOBEL PRIZE TEAM
John Bardeen (1908-1991) (rear left) and Walter Brattain (1902-1987) (right) were members of a research team led by William Shockley (seated) at the Bell Telephone Laboratories. In 1947, they demonstrated the first semiconductor amplifier. Their work was the result of Bell's deliberate policy of searching for new technologies that could improve the telephone system.

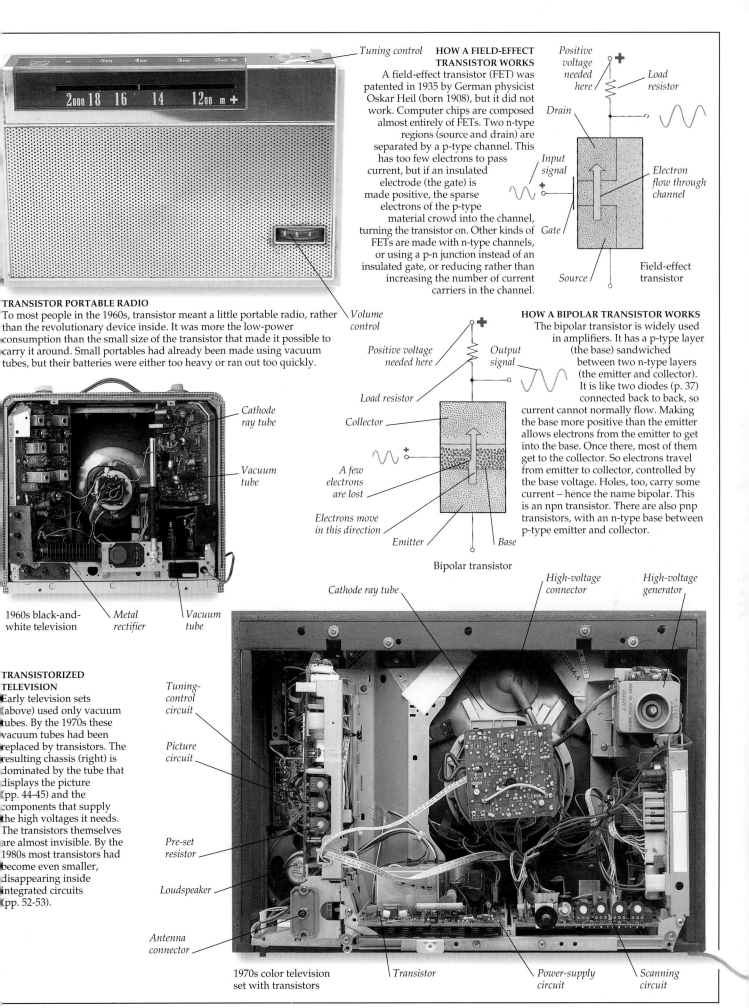

HOW A FIELD-EFFECT TRANSISTOR WORKS

A field-effect transistor (FET) was patented in 1935 by German physicist Oskar Heil (born 1908), but it did not work. Computer chips are composed almost entirely of FETs. Two n-type regions (source and drain) are separated by a p-type channel. This has too few electrons to pass current, but if an insulated electrode (the gate) is made positive, the sparse electrons of the p-type material crowd into the channel, turning the transistor on. Other kinds of FETs are made with n-type channels, or using a p-n junction instead of an insulated gate, or reducing rather than increasing the number of current carriers in the channel.

Positive voltage needed here

Load resistor

Drain

Input signal

Electron flow through channel

Gate

Source

Field-effect transistor

TRANSISTOR PORTABLE RADIO

To most people in the 1960s, transistor meant a little portable radio, rather than the revolutionary device inside. It was more the low-power consumption than the small size of the transistor that made it possible to carry it around. Small portables had already been made using vacuum tubes, but their batteries were either too heavy or ran out too quickly.

Volume control

HOW A BIPOLAR TRANSISTOR WORKS

The bipolar transistor is widely used in amplifiers. It has a p-type layer (the base) sandwiched between two n-type layers (the emitter and collector). It is like two diodes (p. 37) connected back to back, so current cannot normally flow. Making the base more positive than the emitter allows electrons from the emitter to get into the base. Once there, most of them get to the collector. So electrons travel from emitter to collector, controlled by the base voltage. Holes, too, carry some current – hence the name bipolar. This is an npn transistor. There are also pnp transistors, with an n-type base between p-type emitter and collector.

Positive voltage needed here

Output signal

Load resistor

Collector

A few electrons are lost

Electrons move in this direction

Emitter

Base

Bipolar transistor

Cathode ray tube

Vacuum tube

1960s black-and-white television

Metal rectifier

Vacuum tube

Cathode ray tube

High-voltage connector

High-voltage generator

TRANSISTORIZED TELEVISION

Early television sets (above) used only vacuum tubes. By the 1970s these vacuum tubes had been replaced by transistors. The resulting chassis (right) is dominated by the tube that displays the picture (pp. 44-45) and the components that supply the high voltages it needs. The transistors themselves are almost invisible. By the 1980s most transistors had become even smaller, disappearing inside integrated circuits (pp. 52-53).

Tuning-control circuit

Picture circuit

Pre-set resistor

Loudspeaker

Antenna connector

1970s color television set with transistors

Transistor

Power-supply circuit

Scanning circuit

High frequencies

WHEN ELECTROMAGNETIC WAVES ENCOUNTER a circuit that is not much smaller than they are, strange things can happen. As the frequency rises into the microwave region above a billion hertz (the unit of frequency), the wavelength gets close to the size of a circuit board, and the simple idea of a circuit begins to fade away. Conductors start to span parts of the wave that are out of step with each other, so that voltages and currents no longer add up as expected. Passive components misbehave, with resistors turning into inductors, and inductors into capacitors. Active components can stop working altogether. Electronics at these frequencies is almost a different subject: Components and circuits have to be made smaller, or the way waves travel has to be allowed for, or both. Even electrons can be too sluggish for microwaves, so special semiconductors are often needed in microwave amplifiers. But there are good reasons for taming these exotic waves. Microwaves can carry more information. They keep to straight paths, which is useful for linking cities. Unlike longer waves, they can penetrate the Earth's outer atmosphere to allow communication with space.

THE MICROWAVE OVEN
When high-power microwaves became available in the 1940s, workers noticed that they could make things hot. It was American engineer Percy Le Baron Spencer (1894-1970) who in 1945 found a microwave-melted candy in his pocket and conceived the idea of the microwave oven.

Large objects cast shadows

Runway

Airplane

AIRPORT RADAR IMAGE
This is London's Heathrow Airport as seen on a radar at its center. As the frequency of radio waves rises, their wavelength falls, and they begin to behave more like light. With a wavelength of only millimeters, this radar can pick out details of aircraft and buildings. The beam spreads at the edges, making the picture there less clear.

Radar antenna rotates

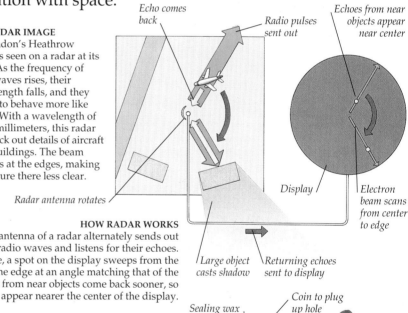

Echo comes back

Radio pulses sent out

Echoes from near objects appear near center

Display

Electron beam scans from center to edge

Large object casts shadow

Returning echoes sent to display

HOW RADAR WORKS
The rotating antenna of a radar alternately sends out short pulses of radio waves and listens for their echoes. After each pulse, a spot on the display sweeps from the center to the edge at an angle matching that of the antenna. Echoes from near objects come back sooner, so appear nearer the center of the display.

RANDALL AND BOOT MAGNETRON
Clear radar images of distant objects demand a high-power source of microwaves. British physicists John Randall (1905-1984) and Harry Boot (1917-1983) of Birmingham University in England put this prototype magnetron together in 1940, using bits and pieces from their laboratory. The magnetron whirled electrons around in the field of a powerful electromagnet (p. 18) to generate waves 4 in (10 cm) long with a power of 40 watts. This is the ancestor of the magnetron that is used to power every microwave oven.

Sealing wax

Coin to plug up hole

Water-cooling tube

Copper anode block inside

PLOTTING AIRCRAFT
Radar is a way of detecting objects and measuring their position by firing bursts of high-frequency radio waves at them and timing the echoes that come back. It was developed from the 1930s onward. This member of Britain's Women's Auxiliary Air Force (WAAF) is plotting targets by radar during World War II (1939-1945).

Connection to vacuum pump

Plate against which one pole of electromagnet fits

1946-107

Water-cooling tube

SATELLITE TELEVISION

The idea of broadcasting from a satellite that appears to stand still in the sky is not new. But only recently has microwave technology become inexpensive and reliable enough to allow an affordable service. Microwaves at frequencies of more than 10 billion hertz are used, which easily penetrate the atmosphere. The domestic satellite television dish is a miniature version of the huge dishes used to beam signals up to satellites (p. 13). The amount of power in the incoming television signal, after its 44,000-mile (70,000-km) journey through space, is unbelievably tiny. But the low-noise block still manages to amplify it and shift its frequency down to something more easily handled by the satellite receiver inside the house.

Perforations in reflector make it less conspicuous

Low-noise block amplifies signal and reduces its frequency

Horn with weather shield

Incoming waves from satellite

Cable supplies power to low-noise block

MICROWAVE REPEATER STATION

Microwaves can carry a lot of information – they are like fine silk compared with the coarse cloth of lower frequencies. Very small reflectors can focus the microwaves into tight beams that form point-to-point telephone, television, and computer links between stations like this one on the Nullarbor Plain in Australia.

Mounting bracket holds dish almost vertical to prevent snow from settling

HIGH POWER KLYSTRON

Many recent developments in electronics make use of specialized types of vacuum tubes invented in the 1930s. They are, for example, the only devices able to deliver enough power for satellite communications. Devices such as this 15-in (40-cm)-high klystron amplifier from a satellite ground station make use of the otherwise awkward fact that microwaves can go through several cycles in the time it takes an electron to travel from cathode to anode (pp. 26-27).

HOW A TV DISH WORKS

The dish gathers microwaves from space and concentrates them into a low-noise block at the top of the cable, where a sophisticated amplifier boosts the very weak signal without adding noise. The block then reduces the frequency of the signal before sending it down the cable to the indoor receiver.

Waves reflected

Horn

Low-noise block

Cable feeds signal to receiver

Signal input

Cooling fin

High-voltage connector

Output waveguide (p.13)

Magnet to prevent electron beam spreading out

Translating useful signals

DAVID HUGHES (1831-1900)
Hughes was born in London but emigrated to America, where he became a professor of music and invented a successful telegraph. Back in London, experimenting with sound, he discovered an effective transducer. It was so sensitive that he thought of it as a sound microscope, and called it the microphone.

IF ELECTRONICS PRODUCED ONLY ELECTRICAL EFFECTS, it would be of limited value. To do useful things, it needs devices that can translate voltages and currents into the sounds, lights, and forces of everyday life. Likewise, electronic devices need the physical world to be translated into electrical signals. Devices that can perform these translations are called transducers. They are able to change the type of energy that is carrying information without changing the information itself. A familiar example is the loudspeaker, which converts electric power into sound. But transducers can now detect everything from radioactivity to smoke and produce effects ranging from ear-splitting sound to gently changing light. To do this, they use a wide range of processes, including electromagnetism, the effect of light on semiconductors, and the variation of resistance with stress and temperature.

Wooden base helps pick up sound

Connecting wires

Loose nail vibrates with sound

Nails stuck with wax

THREE NAILS MAKING SOUND
Hughes discovered that loose electrical contacts are extraordinarily sensitive to vibrations, including sound. This 1878 arrangement of three ordinary nails must rate as one of the world's simplest scientific breakthroughs. Microphones using Hughes's principle are more efficient transducers than Bell's telephone (below). This one was so responsive that, even without electronic amplification, it could detect a fly's footstep. Connected to a modern tape recorder, it will produce an acceptable recording.

THE RADIO MICROPHONE
Perhaps the most famous transducer of them all, this microphone was used by the BBC from 1934 until 1959. Tiny pressure changes caused by sound waves make the aluminum ribbon, less than a thousandth of a millimeter thick, vibrate between the poles of a large magnet. This generates currents through an amplifier that mimic the soundwave accurately as it leaves the cone of the loudspeaker.

BBC-Marconi AXBT ribbon microphone with cover

Wooden case

Currents in wire make diaphragm vibrate

Magnet

Iron diaphragm

EARLY TELEPHONE
The first practical transducer that could deal with a continuously changing signal was Alexander Graham Bell's telephone of 1876. It could convert sound into electromagnetic waves (pp. 12-13) and back again. Vibrations of a thin iron diaphragm set up currents in wires wound around a magnet. Alternatively, currents in the wires could make the diaphragm vibrate. Putting instruments like this at each end of a long wire, Bell made the first effective telephone.

A WORLD SERVICE
The electronic chain that carries voices and music around the world begins and ends with transducers – a microphone in a studio and a loudspeaker in a distant listener's home. This microphone was developed from the ribbon unit (right).

HOW A LOUDSPEAKER WORKS

Most loudspeakers use a cone of paper, fabric, or plastic attached to a moving coil. Currents through the coil create magnetism, which produces forces that push and pull the cone as the currents surge back and forth. The magnetic field is created by a permanent magnet mounted around the end of the coil. The cone in turn pushes and pulls the air, launching waves that we can hear as sound.

Centering spider stops speech coil moving sideways

Rubber surround

Plastic cone

Permanent magnet

Gap contains magnetic field

Aluminum speech coil

Metal chassis

Pole pieces create magnetic field around ribbon

Permanent magnet

Aluminum ribbon responds to sound

Pole piece

Connection to ribbon

Front panel of speaker enclosure

Screw for fixing to stand

Ribbon microphone without cover

Crossover filter inductors

HI-FI SPEAKER
The design of loudspeakers is exceptionally difficult because the ear is able to detect very slight errors in the translation from electrical signals to sound. This loudspeaker of 1974 uses separate transducers for low and high frequencies. A crossover filter (pp. 34-35) ensures that each transducer is fed only the signals it needs.

High-frequency transducer

Crossover filter capacitors

Magnet

Low-frequency transducer

Reset button

LCD temperature read-out

Temperature-sensing metal tip

Safety cover

SENSING LIGHT
Without transducers, street lamps have to be turned on and off by hand or by a time switch. Electronic sensors that incorporate light-sensitive transistors are now cheap enough to fit on every lamp post. They do not need adjusting for the varying times of sunset and sunrise, and the lamp even comes on in daytime in bad weather in response to the light conditions at the time.

RESPONSE TO HEAT
At the tip of this electronic thermometer is a tiny heat-sensitive resistor that warms up when placed in the mouth. An electronic chip in the body of the instrument converts the changing resistance to a temperature reading. It works faster than traditional thermometers and contains far less of the potentially dangerous mercury.

The visual connection

LOOKING AT A PIECE OF ELECTRONIC EQUIPMENT, the first thing most people notice is the display. This is no accident. Displays are there to attract attention, to communicate. Although progress has been made with electronic speech recognition, most interaction with electronic systems is visual. Their displays range from a computer screen to a simple light that warns you that something is switched on. Although computer graphics can look impressively modern, they are usually seen on a device that started life in 1897 – the cathode ray tube (CRT). Despite efforts to find a slimmer, cheaper alternative, the CRT still shows the best pictures. It offers more detail, higher brightness, and can be viewed over a wider angle than any of its competitors. But if you do not need pictures, there are plenty of alternatives. Liquid crystal displays (LCDs) use almost no power. Light-emitting diodes (LEDs) or electromechanical displays can make large, clear signs. Vacuum fluorescent displays use the same principle as the CRT to produce the glowing green numbers seen on video recorders.

LARGER THAN LIFE
The screens of cathode ray tubes (CRTs) cannot be made very big, although small CRTs, when used with lenses, can project images 6 ft 6 in (2 m) wide, and projectors using an arc lamp controlled by a CRT can do even better. But discharge tubes like the ones used in advertising signs can form a huge screen. Electronics sends a different bit of the picture to each of the thousands of red, green, and blue tubes. This type of display has become a regular feature of international sporting events, giving each spectator a close-up view. Here runners are seen lining up for the start of the marathon at the Los Angeles Olympics of 1984.

Connection for high voltage to accelerate electrons toward screen

COLOR TELEVISION TUBE
This tube is really three cathode ray tubes in one, showing pictures in red, green, and blue. Together these three colors can match almost any color. The tube has three electron guns in the neck and a metal shadow mask near the screen, positioned so that any point on the screen receives electrons from only one gun. All the points that receive electrons from the red gun are coated with a chemical phosphor that glows red when electrons hit it, and likewise for green and blue. The result is a full-color picture made from stripes of just three colors.

Connecting pin for picture signals

Three electron guns hidden inside shared anode

Movable magnet adjusts color purity and lines up three pictures

Scanning coil sweeps electron beams across screen magnetically

Shadow mask made from tensioned vertical wires

Phosphor stripes coated on glass

LONGINES CLOCK

Digital displays were a rarity in the early 1960s, when this clock was made. The numbers are produced by Nixie tubes based on neon lamps of the sort still used to indicate when electrical appliances are switched on. Control logic (pp. 50-51), connected to electrodes inside, makes the orange discharge form around one of ten display electrodes shaped to show the digits 0-9.

Hours | *Nixie tube* | *Minutes* | *Seconds*

Power cord

AMSTERDAM AIRPORT

Electromechanical devices, like this one at Amsterdam's international airport in the Netherlands, make large, clear displays. They have the advantage of using power only when the message is actually changing. At other times the mechanism retains the last message sent.

tijd time	vlucht flight	naar to
11:35	KL 501	ATHENE
12:00	KL 119	LONDON HEATHROW
12:45	CI 062	TAIPEI DHAHRAN
13:00	CP 046	FRANKFURT
13:00	KL 611	CHICAGO
13:15	KL 327	PARIS DE GAULLE
13:15	KL 553	CAIRO
13:30	KL 121	LONDON HEATHROW
13:30	KL 691	TORONTO
14:00	CP 051	TORONTO
14:15	CP 045	VANCOUVER CALGARY
15:00	GA 893	JAKARTA ROME
15:00	KL 6357	GOOSEBAY
15:35	SR 789	GENEVE
15:45	KL 2525	HERAKLION
16:00	KL 127	LONDON HEATHROW
16:15	SR 793	ZURICH
16:20	TK 954	ANKARA ISTANBUL
16:45	KL 347	ROME FIUMICINO
16:55	KL 315	ZURICH
17:00	KL 123	LONDON HEATHROW

BODY SCANNING

Computer technology for business, science, and medicine depends on displays to link people with machines. A powerful computer in this scanner combines many X-ray measurements to form a detailed picture of the patient's body. Without the color display that reveals the picture to the radiographer, its work would be much less useful.

Transparent electrode

Light

Top polarizer

Polarization of light twisted through right angle by liquid crystal

No voltage applied

Liquid crystal molecules

Bottom polarizer

Glass plate

Mirror

LCD display OFF

PORTABLE DISPLAY

Liquid crystal displays have no rivals for portable equipment because they consume almost no power. More advanced displays incorporate transistors within the monitor itself to look after each of the thousands of picture elements, simplifying the circuits needed to control them. By making each point of the screen a cluster of red, green, and blue elements, full-color pictures can be displayed.

LCD monitor is backlit

Lid folds down for carrying

Wires connecting to monitor inside the hinge

Keyboard

HOW LCD WORKS

Liquid crystals are liquids with a regular structure. Some can polarize light, like sunglasses. Trapped between glass plates with special surfaces, their molecules lie flat and form a twisted path that guides light through a pair of crossed polarizers. But when a voltage between the plates makes the molecules stand on end, they can no longer guide the light, and the display turns dark.

Coated surface makes molecules line up with direction of polarizer

Voltage applied

No polarizing effect so light blocked

Mirror

LCD display ON

Analog and digital

E LECTRONIC SYSTEMS CAN HANDLE INFORMATION in one of two forms: Signals may vary smoothly and continuously, like the rapid variations of air pressure that we hear as sound, or they may consist of only a limited number of symbols, like the letters of a message. Analog electronics smoothly translates varying quantities into smoothly varying signals, while digital systems deal with definite symbols. Although digital systems obey the fundamental principles of analog electronics, their information content is coded in binary – on-off or plus-minus form. This obviously suits things like letters or numbers. It is not so obvious that digital electronics can also handle analog signals, but many smoothly varying quantities can be reduced to numbers and then treated like any other numerical data. This is advantageous. Digital signals can be manipulated by computers and are also less affected by interference.

INTRODUCING BINARY
German philosopher and mathematician Gottfried Leibniz (1646-1716) brought the significance of the binary system to the attention of other mathematicians in 1703. He was mainly interested in it as proof that the world was created by God. The system is a way of writing numbers using only two symbols. Because electronic switches flip between just two states, it is the best way of representing numbers in digital electronic equipment.

HOW BINARY WORKS
Traditional kitchen scales use weights of 8, 4, 2, and 1 units. The weights making up a given quantity can be recorded using a 1 to show a weight is needed and a 0 to show it is not. The weights making up 14 units would be written 1110, meaning use 8, 4, and 2 but not 1. The binary system works in just this way. Binary digits – bits – show which fixed numbers must be added to make a given number. The last bit on the right shows whether or not 1 is needed. Bits to the left of this indicate the need for 2, 4, and so on. The number 25 becomes 11001, with the bits standing for 16, 8, and 1 set to 1 because these numbers add up to 25. Since 4 and 2 are not needed, their bits are set to 0.

Adding flour until the scales balance gives the required quantity

SAMPLING THE ACTION
Moving pictures are an illusion built up from still pictures. Rapid action can reveal this, as when wagon wheels appear to roll backward in the movies. Digital sampling also works by taking snapshots. An analog signal (top) is measured or sampled at regular intervals and the measurements are expressed in binary code to form a digital signal (center). The conversion is never exact, and if the sampling is done too slowly (below), the decoded signal may be completely misleading, as with the wagon wheels.

Sample value

Digital signal

Sample value

Misleading signal

Weights representing desired quantity placed on scale first

2 unit weight

4 unit weight

8 unit weight

Record groove — ⟍   ⟋ _Stylus tip_

NOISY SURFACE

Analog recording reigned supreme in home electronics until the 1980s. Long-playing records (LPs), molded in vinyl plastic, appeared in the late 1940s. They were a direct development from earlier records, which had coarser grooves and a higher playing speed. This scanning electron micrograph of modern record grooves shows how they capture every nuance of the original sound wave. But because the shape of the wave is translated directly into the shape of the surface, any damage must appear as noise – usually a loud thump as the stylus runs over a scratch. This inability to distinguish between signal and noise is a basic limitation of analog systems.

ALEC REEVES (1902-1971)

The idea of converting speech to digital code came to British telephone engineer Alec Reeves as early as 1937. He was working on systems that could send many telephone calls down one cable to link exchanges in two different cities. He showed that sampling and analog-to-digital conversion could reduce telephone calls to a stream of on-off pulses. Unlike analog signals, these pulses would hardly be affected by interference from other channels sharing the same cable. This would allow a cable to carry more calls without annoying cross talk. His pulse code modulation technique had to wait until the 1970s for electronic devices advanced enough to make it practical. It is now used for long-distance links everywhere.

CONVERTING SIGNALS

A modern telephone exchange is really a specialized computer. It is able to treat calls as if they were computer data because every call passes through an analog-to-digital converter before the exchange sends it on its way. A digital link speeds it to the destination exchange, where a digital-to-analog converter recreates the original signal before passing it to the telephone being called.

BETTER SOUND QUALITY

A compact disc is smaller than an LP, plays more than twice as long with better sound, and is unaffected by minor damage. All this is possible because the sound is converted into a string of digital codes, which appear on the disc as microscopic pits that can be read by a laser beam. A complicated coding system ensures that there is usually enough data elsewhere on the disc to fill in any parts of the recording made unreadable by scratches.

CONVERTING QUANTITIES

A fish can be any weight. Its weight is an analog quantity. Matching it with weights whose total can only change in fixed steps is an analog-to-digital conversion. Weighing flour (left) is a digital-to-analog conversion, because the fixed weights are balanced by a continuously variable weight of flour.

Fish placed on scale first

Weights added to balance fish, thus representing its weight as a definite number

Signals and codes

People everywhere make similar sounds when they talk, but this does not mean they can all understand each other. They can communicate only if they share a code that links sounds to meanings – a language. In the same way, electronic systems all use similar voltages, currents, and waves, but successful communication between them demands that they use an agreed-upon code. Most television sets will only work with signals conforming to a particular national standard. In another country, where television is coded differently, they will not produce recognizable pictures. Unlike human languages, electronic codes vary widely in efficiency. Some earlier codes are inefficient and use a wider range of transmitted frequencies (pp. 14-15) than is really necessary. This is because efficient coding often demands computing power that has only really been available since the advent of the microprocessor (pp. 56-57).

GETTING THE MESSAGE
People also need a common code if they are to communicate. In an internatonal game, the referee's whistle is not always enough. The card system offers a clearly agreed code. When a player sees the yellow warning card, he gets the message, whatever his native language.

Dash

Dot

MORSE TAPE
Early communication systems needed skilled operators to interpret the language of primitive machines. This tape was produced by a Morse inker that simply marked the received dots and dashes on a strip of paper. A trained clerk was needed to translate the code into ordinary writing that customers could read.

WHEATSTONE TAPE PUNCH
The best-known communication code is the one devised by Samuel Morse (p. 24), although it is now little used. It was highly successful because the more common letters are represented by shorter sequences of dots and dashes, reducing the time taken to send messages. The code is simple enough for machines like this one, made by Charles Wheatstone (p. 24) around 1858, to record it as holes in paper tape. In this form it could be transmitted automatically, allowing fuller use to be made of the telegraph cables.

Paper tape

Tape reel

Punch makes holes in paper tape

Key

Buffer

RADIO INVENTOR
American engineer Edwin Armstrong (1890-1954) is pictured here with a radio receiver of his own design. He was the inventor of two essential building blocks of radio – oscillators (p. 33) and frequency changers (p. 35). In 1933 he also invented a system offering clear sound with a quiet background – frequency modulation (FM). It made Armstrong a millionaire, but in 1954, depressed by people trying to steal his ideas, he took his own life.

Carrier wave

Tips of wave give shape of sound wave

COMMUNICATION THEORY

In 1948 the American engineer Claude Shannon (b. 1916) developed a way of measuring information in communications systems. It was based on the idea that the more unexpected a signal, the more information it conveys. He also developed a way of calculating the maximum rate that information can be sent through a given channel. His work sets out the fundamental rules within which communications engineers must operate. It also allows them to see how efficient a code is by checking its rate of transmission against the theoretical limit.

Spectrum contains many frequencies

AMPLITUDE MODULATION

A radio wave can be received from far away, but in itself says only that the transmitter is switched on. To convey useful information, the steady carrier wave must be modulated in some way. Amplitude modulation (AM), displayed here on an oscilloscope, transmits the shape of a sound wave as a variation in the height (amplitude) of the wave from above and below the average line.

No signal here

FREQUENCY MODULATION

Frequency modulation (FM) is another way of varying a carrier wave to convey information. The shape of a sound wave is transmitted by varying the frequency, rather than the strength of the wave. The modulated carrier has a complex spectrum occupying a wide range of frequencies, but it makes up for this by being highly resistant to interference.

AM ON A SPECTRUM ANALYZER

All radio transmissions contain many frequencies (pp. 14-15). Other stations have to avoid these frequencies if there is to be no interference. Amplitude modulation is inefficient because, as this spectrum analyzer picture shows, both halves of its spectrum are exactly the same shape (although one is reversed), wasting frequencies that other stations could use.

Repeated information

Some frequencies have low power

Thinnest line reads as 1

READING A BAR CODE

The stripes of a bar code represent a number that identifies a particular product and pack. The code is standardized so that machines all over the world can read it. In the most widely used type, each digit is represented by stripes totaling 7 units wide. The thinnest lines and spaces are 1 unit wide and the thicker ones up to 4 units wide. The digit codes are not based on the simple binary system (pp. 46-47), and the code for a particular digit varies with its position in the number. This helps prevent errors.

7 80863 185779

Each digit code is 7 units wide

Thinnest space reads as 0

BAR CODE READER

Bar code readers can be fixed or hand held. Fixed readers normally use a laser to scan the code, but hand-held models sometimes incorporate a device rather like a tiny television camera. In either case the result is a string of on-off pulses that can be decoded by a computer. A beep signals successful decoding. The long stripes allow the code to be read at an angle (multiple laser beams also help with this), while clever coding helps the machine detect errors and read the code upside down.

Bar code

Light from reader

Logical rules

Early computers were sometimes called electronic brains because they amazed people with their ability to solve logical problems. In fact, computers are nothing like human brains, which can easily solve problems that defeat computers but are often confused by logical puzzles. Boolean algebra enables us to take such problems one step at a time and reach the right conclusion. This is just what computers do, but millions of times faster than humans can. Engineers give computers their power by building the rules of logic into electronic circuits called gates, which are switches that turn on or off when presented with the right combination of inputs. Digital circuits formed by connecting gates together can be made to obey any desired rule, as long as it is completely clear.

GEORGE BOOLE (1815-1864)
British mathematician George Boole was entirely self-taught. He never earned a degree, yet became a professor of mathematics and in 1854 published his algebra – a way of combining symbols that perfectly expresses the rules of logic. Using this system, complicated rules can be written clearly and often simplified.

VENN DIAGRAM
The basic Boolean operations are AND, OR, and NOT. Pictures like this, based on the type of diagram invented around 1880 by the British logician John Venn (1834-1923), can be used to illustrate these operations. Out of many possible shapes and colors, one circle contains only cubes (of several colors), while the other contains only red bricks (of several shapes). Where the circles overlap, the bricks must be red AND cubes. The two circles together contain bricks that are red OR cubes. In the area outside the circles, the bricks are NOT red AND NOT cubes.

THE LANGUAGE OF LOGIC

The basic Boolean operations are AND ($\cap$), OR ($\cup$), and NOT ($\overline{}$). These and others can be carried out electronically by logic gates. Each gate has a special symbol used in drawing the diagrams that show how the gates are to be connected. Some gates are shown below with Boolean equations giving the rules they follow.

A, B → C	AND gate:	$C = A \cap B$
A, B → C	OR gate:	$C = A \cup B$
A → C	Inverter:	$C = \overline{A}$
A, B → C	NAND gate:	$C = \overline{A \cap B}$
A, B → C	NOR gate:	$C = \overline{A \cup B}$

Boolean algebra can be used to write rules that will be obeyed by logic gates connected together to give the same Boolean expression. A car seat-belt-warning device might obey the rule "if there is weight on the seat and the belt is not fastened, flash the warning light," or more simply, "light = weight AND NOT fastened." Boolean algebra allows the corresponding statement $L = W \cap \overline{F}$ to be changed to $\overline{L} = \overline{W} \cup F$, which says that the light should stay off if there is no weight, or the belt is fastened.

The seat-belt circuit would look like this: W, F → L

or, using a different set of gates, like this: W, F → L

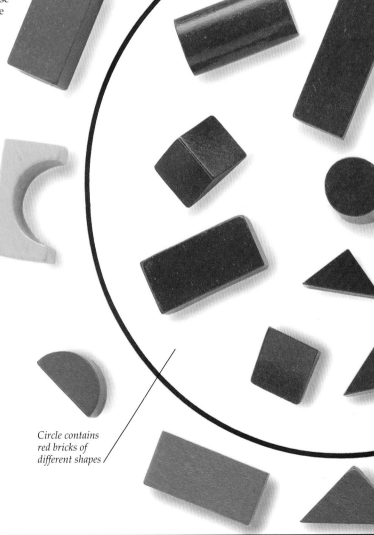

Circle contains red bricks of different shapes

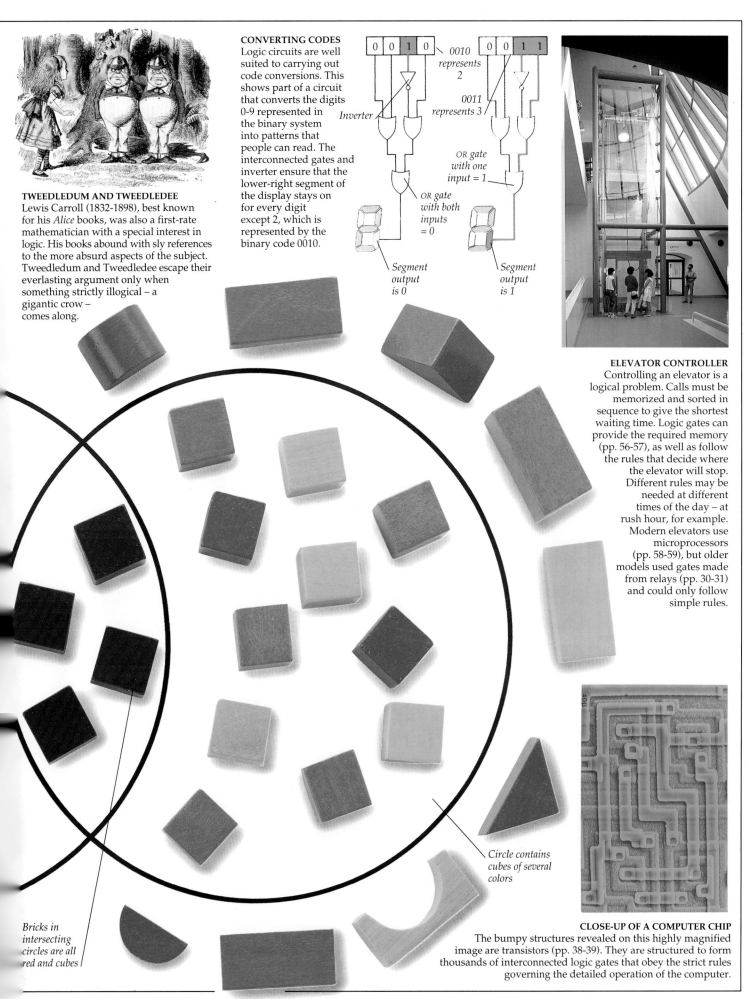

TWEEDLEDUM AND TWEEDLEDEE
Lewis Carroll (1832-1898), best known for his *Alice* books, was also a first-rate mathematician with a special interest in logic. His books abound with sly references to the more absurd aspects of the subject. Tweedledum and Tweedledee escape their everlasting argument only when something strictly illogical – a gigantic crow – comes along.

CONVERTING CODES
Logic circuits are well suited to carrying out code conversions. This shows part of a circuit that converts the digits 0-9 represented in the binary system into patterns that people can read. The interconnected gates and inverter ensure that the lower-right segment of the display stays on for every digit except 2, which is represented by the binary code 0010.

0010 represents 2

0011 represents 3

Inverter

OR gate with one input = 1

OR gate with both inputs = 0

Segment output is 0

Segment output is 1

ELEVATOR CONTROLLER
Controlling an elevator is a logical problem. Calls must be memorized and sorted in sequence to give the shortest waiting time. Logic gates can provide the required memory (pp. 56-57), as well as follow the rules that decide where the elevator will stop. Different rules may be needed at different times of the day – at rush hour, for example. Modern elevators use microprocessors (pp. 58-59), but older models used gates made from relays (pp. 30-31) and could only follow simple rules.

Circle contains cubes of several colors

Bricks in intersecting circles are all red and cubes

CLOSE-UP OF A COMPUTER CHIP
The bumpy structures revealed on this highly magnified image are transistors (pp. 38-39). They are structured to form thousands of interconnected logic gates that obey the strict rules governing the detailed operation of the computer.

Integrated circuits

UNTIL THE 1960S ELECTRONICS ENGINEERS were limited in what they could do by the size of vacuum tubes and transistors. Engineers have always sought ways to pack more into less. A first attempt at an integrated circuit was made by Siegmund Loewe in 1926. The first semiconductor integrated circuit was made by Jack Kilby in 1958. It incorporated several transistors on one piece of semiconductor, but there was no way of connecting them together except by hand. The answer was the planar process of 1959, which etches transistors into a silicon surface using photographic techniques (pp. 54-55). The silicon over their active regions is converted into inert oxide or nitride. The resulting transistors are tough and flat, making connection easy. By 1962, with further development of the planar process to connect transistors together with metal tracks, the first truly integrated circuits, commonly known as chips, were finding their way into electronics.

Glass tube

Tuning coil

Tuning control

EARLY INTEGRATED CIRCUIT
German engineer Siegmund Loewe (1885-1962) developed several vacuum tubes that included in one envelope nearly all the components – resistors, capacitors and diodes – needed to make a radio. The base of this compact receiver provides only variable capacitors and an interchangeable coil for tuning. Everything else is in the tube.

Recording level meter

Manual rewind handle

Pinch wheel

1950s TAPE RECORDER
The change in scale brought about by integrated circuits is well illustrated by the way the tape recorder has shrunk in size over the years. Improvements in electric motors and the development of compact cassettes have also helped. This professional tape machine was a triumph of miniaturization when it was made in the early 1950s. It substituted some of the first transistors for the diodes of previous models. But its amplifiers alone occupy more space than an entire personal stereo of 1990. (The two machines are shown here in proportion.)

Tape spool

Loudspeaker

JACK KILBY (B. 1923)

In 1952, Kilby, an American electronics engineer, realized that because transistors were small, the space taken up by their connecting wires was significant. Packing a lot of separate transistors into a small space produced an unworkable maze. In 1958, he demonstrated the first circuit – including resistors, capacitors, and transistors – ever made from a single piece of semiconductor.

Earphone wire doubles as antenna

CARD RADIO

This Japanese pocket radio, made in 1983, has all the electronics needed for an FM receiver integrated into one slim chip, mounted in a case the size of a credit card. The chip itself occupies only a fraction of the space – most of the space is used to accommodate batteries and the large tuning capacitor, which in more recent designs would be replaced by a tiny diode (pp. 36-37).

Light-emitting diode (LED) display

Sinclair Executive

Earphone

Tuning control operates variable capacitor

Frequency scale

SINCLAIR CALCULATOR

This pocket calculator was made in Britain by Sinclair, one of the first companies to offer miniaturized electronic equipment. Calculators became widely available in the early 1970s as one of the first fruits of integrated-circuit technology. They swept aside traditional calculating aids, like the slide rule and abacus (p. 8), that had been used for generations. They squeezed computing power, which formerly required a large cabinet into the space of a shirt pocket.

Key pad

Inside the package

Integrated circuits can do jobs ranging from precision amplification to high-speed calculation. But they all look much the same on the outside, and even breaking the package open reveals little. With working parts as small as a thousandth of a millimeter wide, the features that distinguish one from another can be seen only under a powerful microscope.

Battery compartment

MAGNIFIED CHIP

Only through a powerful microscope is it possible to get some idea of the intricacies etched on the surface of an integrated circuit.

Volume control

Recording level display

Cassette

Noise reduction

Plastic package

Pins

1990s PERSONAL STEREO

With the arrival of the truly personal stereo, listening on the move has become a major craze. This professional machine depends on integrated circuits to cram advanced facilities – stereo recording, noise reduction, and provision for different kinds of tape – into a pocket-sized package.

PACKAGED INTEGRATED CHIP

The problem of interconnection still exists even when many transistors have been integrated into one chip. In this simple integrated circuit, the actual slice of silicon inside (right) is dwarfed by the packaging needed to accommodate the connections to the pins that plug into a printed circuit board (pp. 22-23).

Silicon chip

Making microchips

Microchips are among the most intricate devices ever made. Although the largest integrated circuit is only the size of a thumbnail, a drawing showing everything on it would be bigger than a detailed map of a major city. This level of complexity allows integrated circuits to do jobs that once required rooms full of equipment. Designing and making such devices is a formidable task. It is easy to dream up new things for chips to do, but intensive effort, assisted by computers – themselves made from chips – is needed to work out the details of the design. The manufacturing process needs skill, too. Working on the microscopic scale of these devices requires enormous care.

CHECKING THE PATTERN
Although computers carry out much of the design process for chips, the resulting patterns are checked by designers after being printed out on a machine resembling a gigantic color photocopier.

MANUFACTURING SEQUENCE
Silicon wafers (p. 36) are turned into integrated circuits by a sequence of operations that includes masking, etching, diffusion, ion implantation (bombarding the wafer with electrically charged atoms), and metallization (creating tracks to link the components). Each wafer may become a hundred or more chips. Just a few of the steps are shown here. Things can go wrong at any stage. A speck of dust can spoil a chip. A processing error can ruin a whole batch of wafers. Getting a good yield of working microchips requires meticulous attention to detail and can make the difference between the success or failure of a business.

Different color for each pattern

Transparent plastic sheet

1 SUPERIMPOSED PATTERNS
Extensive checking is essential before embarking on the costly process of chip making. At the early design stages, computers check out the logical design and electrical characteristics of the proposed chip to pinpoint any weaknesses. It is also important that the many superimposed patterns that form the chip line up accurately. For simple chips, transparencies like these can be laid on top of each other to help spot any errors.

Control pattern used for testing

2 PHOTO MASK
A photo mask is used to create a microscopic stencil on the wafer. The wafer is first exposed to oxygen to coat it with impermeable oxide. The photographic process then creates the stencil through which the oxide is etched away. This leaves areas of naked silicon ready to receive the next treatment.

3 DIFFUSING IMPURITIES

Wafers are heated to high temperatures and exposed to chemical compounds that contain the impurity atoms (p. 37) needed to form the parts of the circuit being made at this stage. Batches of wafers are fed into a furnace where the atoms will diffuse only into those parts of the surface left exposed by the previous masking and etching operations. The wafers will go through many such masking, etching, and diffusion steps before the circuit is complete. Control of time and temperature are critical in diffusion, as they have a significant effect on the properties of the finished transistors on the chip. The microscopic scale of these devices requires workers to operate in ultraclean rooms, and be masked and gowned like surgeons, because the tiniest speck of dust could prevent a transistor from being formed properly.

4 TESTING PROBES

After the entire sequence of steps has been carried out, (including several steps such as metallization that are not shown here), the finished wafers are ready for testing. Every wafer includes a number of control chips that can be tested to ensure that all the steps have been carried out correctly. Individual chips are put through a test cycle. Any that fail are marked for rejection. The tests are carried out by delicate probes operated by a computer. A low failure rate at this stage is crucial if the manufacturing company is to make a profit from the chip.

5 BONDING ON WIRES

Individual chips cut from the wafer are now given their links with the outside world. Using a process of cold welding, extremely fine gold wires are bonded onto tiny pads formed around the edges of the chip during the metallization stage. A microscope is needed to line up the chip with the bonding equipment. The automatic process is monitored through the microscope on a television screen. The other ends of the wires will be bonded to the pins that connect the chip to a circuit board.

Plastic packaging

6 PACKAGING THE CHIP

The chip and its connecting wires are enclosed in a tough plastic or ceramic package. Ceramic packages are used when the chip generates or must withstand high temperatures. This is a small-scale integration chip.

Pin

7 PART OF A SYSTEM

The packaged chips are sent out to other manufacturers to be built into their products. Integrated circuits of all sizes are needed to make a working system. The large, complex chips do the bulk of the work, but simpler chips, sometimes collectively known as glue logic, are needed to link these together and control them. The largest chips may each contain more than a million transistors.

Connector where board plugs into computer

Chips installed in a printed circuit board from a personal computer

Large communications chip

Small glue logic chip

How electronic devices remember

THE APPARENT INTELLIGENCE OF COMPUTERS depends largely on the simple ability to remember. Computers do what they are told, but to follow instructions they have to remember them. As they work, they also need to refer to stored information and remember what they have done so far. The kind of memory required depends on the kind and quantity of information involved. Programs or data may take up a lot of space and need to be stored for years. A keyboard remembers most keystrokes for a few thousandths of a second. Data the computer works on may have to go into or out of memory in ten-millionths of a second. Specialized devices exist for all these purposes.

Records

NON-STOP MUSIC
Besides containing a mass of information stored as music on discs, a jukebox has a memory that stores users' requests. Without this, people would have to wait until one record had finished before selecting the next. Memories of this kind are called buffers. They are needed wherever two devices that work at different speeds have to communicate. Early jukeboxes like this one had mechanical memories. Modern machines have fully electronic memories.

FLIP-FLOP SWITCH
A push-push switch like the one on this desk lamp is a mechanical flip-flop. It can remember just one bit of information – whether it turned the light on or off the last time it was pushed. Whatever it did last time, it does the opposite this time. A set of electronic flip-flops of this kind, with the state of each flip-flop representing one binary digit, can be used for counting.

Codes for selection

Selector buttons

Pressing the switch gives opposite action to the last time

Loudspeaker

Basic memory systems

The simplest electronic memory element, the flip-flop, was invented as long ago as 1919. It is basically two amplifiers, each with its output connected to the other's input. Thousands of flip-flops together can form random-access memory (RAM). More compact dynamic RAM chips (DRAMs) use capacitors (pp. 20-21) to store information. RAM is needed where data must be stored as well as retrieved, though the data are lost when they are switched off. Read-only memory (ROM), whose contents are fixed during manufacture, is ideal for the programs of microprocessor-controlled machines (pp. 58-59). For sheer storage capacity, much slower magnetic disks beat all these easily.

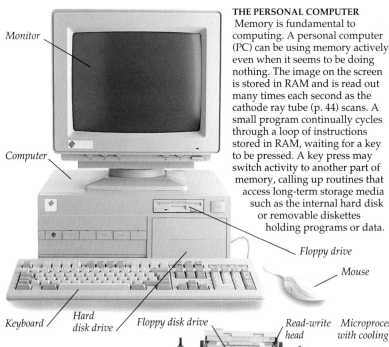

Monitor

Computer

Keyboard

Hard disk drive

Floppy disk drive

Floppy drive

Mouse

THE PERSONAL COMPUTER
Memory is fundamental to computing. A personal computer (PC) can be using memory actively even when it seems to be doing nothing. The image on the screen is stored in RAM and is read out many times each second as the cathode ray tube (p. 44) scans. A small program continually cycles through a loop of instructions stored in RAM, waiting for a key to be pressed. A key press may switch activity to another part of memory, calling up routines that access long-term storage media such as the internal hard disk or removable diskettes holding programs or data.

Memory chip

Edge connectors plug into slots in computer

Disk controller

Crystal controls timing

DISK CONTROLLER BOARD
Computers contain specialized circuit boards that deal with jobs presenting a heavy work-load. Once the computer has given a task to such a board, it is free to work on something else. This speeds up the system, but the specialized board has to remember all the details. This board from a PC feeds data from the microprocessor to the disk drives. These work slowly, so a large buffer memory is needed on the board.

Drive motor

Read-write head

Microprocessor with cooling fan

RAM

Power supply

Slots for extra boards to extend capabilities

INSIDE THE COMPUTER
Looking into this computer, the floppy disk drive is easily seen. It works a little like a compact disc player (pp. 46-47), but uses magnetic, not optical, patterns on the surface of removable disks. Hidden underneath is the fixed or hard disk, which works in much the same way but can store a lot more information. The microprocessor (pp. 58-59) also contains substantial amounts of memory. As well as having registers that hold the data actually being worked on, it maintains a store of recently used instructions for rapid reuse.

Disk coated with magnetic material

Read-write head

Track selector mechanism

Arm

STORING INFORMATION
Hard disks can store tens of millions of bytes (groups of eight binary digits) and retrieve data in a few thousandths of a second. The mechanism is like an agile record player. A magnetic read-write head at the end of the arm is guided by information in a directory stored on the disk itself. Data are stored in narrow concentric tracks divided into sectors. The arm moves to a track, then reads the wanted sector of the spinning disk as it passes.

EPROM CHIP
In a complex memory chip, logic (pp. 50-51) selects the cells that are to be accessed. Groups of cells each have a number, their address. The computer sends an address to the chip, which then sends back the data held at that address or stores new data there. This erasable programmable read-only memory (EPROM) chip cannot store new data. Until erased by ultraviolet light, it holds information permanently as electric charges.

DRAM CHIP
Dynamic random access memory (DRAM) chips store information as the presence or absence of charge in microscopic capacitors. This technique gives very small memory cells, allowing millions of binary digits (p. 46) to be stored on one chip. These memories are called dynamic because the capacitors are rather leaky, requiring each cell to be read and rewritten several hundred times a second. The surface of this chip has been enlarged to 4,000 times its actual size.

Microprocessors

As INTEGRATED CIRCUITS BECAME LARGER in the 1970s, they began to present a problem. Bigger circuits are more expensive to design, are usually more specialized and so have a smaller market. What was needed was one circuit that could do many different tasks. The answer was the microprocessor – a circuit that could read and act on coded instructions. By storing lists of instructions – programs – in an electronic memory, users could make the same chip do a variety of jobs. The microprocessor is the brain of a computer on a single chip. It uses logic (pp. 50-51) to decode instructions and manipulate data as directed. The results can be stored in memory or sent to other devices such as monitors or printers. Although revolutionary when it appeared in 1971, the first microprocessor was slow, offered limited memory access, and could only handle words made up of four binary digits (p. 46). Modern processors can handle 32-bit words, access megabytes of memory, and complete an instruction in a few ten-millionths of a second. Even faster digital signal processors are available for specialized tasks, like sending pictures through telephone lines.

COMPUTER ARCHITECTURE
The basic structure of most microprocessors owes much to the work of Hungarian-born American mathematician John von Neumann (1903-1957). Working on early electronic computers in the 1940s, he realized that their instructions and data could both be stored in the same memory, simplifying the structure. Faster but less versatile digital signal processors (DSPs) use separate instruction and data memories to maximize speed.

MICROPROCESSING STAGES
A microprocessor system used to control equipment is basically a small computer, although its program cannot usually be changed by the user. The microprocessor in these scales (below) normally cycles through an instruction loop that continually converts data from the strain gauge and analog-to-digital (A-to-D) converter (pp. 46-47) to a displayed weight. But it will respond to an interrupt caused by the user pressing a button, either to change the units of weight or to store the weight of a container in random-access memory (pp. 56-57) for subtraction from the displayed readings.

Food to be weighed

Force

Strain gauge

Voltage

A-to-D converter

Binary code for weight

Binary code for voltage

Display driver

Micro- processor

Memory

Instructions and data

Interrupt controller

Interrupt information

Voltages to operate display

Button push signal

Displayed weight

Food being weighed

Weight display

Unit change button

SMART SCALES
Microprocessors can make electronic equipment more intelligent and easier to use. These scales are a simple example. The processor not only does the arithmetic required to convert the output of a transducer (pp. 42-43) into a weight reading. It can also convert the reading to alternative units or alter its zero reading by subtracting the weight of a container. The instructions that control it are held in a read-only memory (pp. 56-57).

Zero button

AZZLING MICROCHIP

he apparently blank
urface of this
icroprocessor chip
onceals hundreds of
ousands of
icroscopic electronic
omponents with
orking parts as small
 one-thousandth of a
illimeter wide. These
rm circuits that
clude a counter to
ep through programs,
gisters (single-word
emories) to hold data
om memory or from
lculations, an
struction decoder, an
cumulator in which
rithmetic or logical results are built
p, and an arithmetic logic unit that
es the actual work of combining and
ansforming data.

ACKAGED MICROPROCESSOR

dvanced microprocessors need a lot of pins for the buses
roups of wires carrying binary words) that connect them to
emory and other devices, so even a large microprocessor
ip is small compared with the connections and packaging
at surround it. This package is 2 in (50 mm) square. The
5 in (12 mm) square microprocessor inside repeats a
cle of retrieving, decoding, and executing
structions millions of times each second.
 can also deal with an interrupt
. 58), then return to what it
as doing.

*rray of pins fits
to circuit board*

*Chip sealed under
metal cover*

ISUAL EAR

icroprocessors have
rned theory into reality
r many professions.
eech therapists can
se this equipment to
elp someone with
npaired hearing
nprove their speech.
 creates pictures of
e sounds the
atient makes,
rawing on ideas
vailable for many
ears but impractical
ntil now.

ELECTRONIC LEARNING

Very large-scale integration (pp. 54-55) has given
children computing power once available only to
scientists. Built into the read-only memory (ROM)
of this microprocessor-controlled educational toy is
not only a long list of words to spell but also
several game programs that make learning fun.

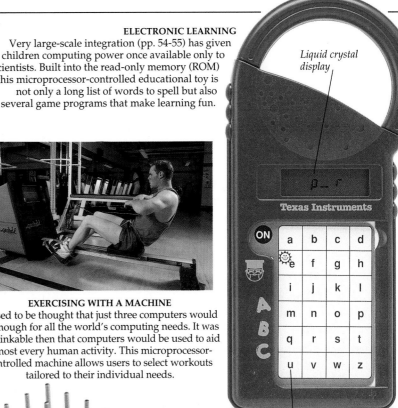

*Liquid crystal
display*

Texas Instruments

*Interchangeable cards
for different games*

EXERCISING WITH A MACHINE

It used to be thought that just three computers would
be enough for all the world's computing needs. It was
unthinkable then that computers would be used to aid
almost every human activity. This microprocessor-
controlled machine allows users to select workouts
tailored to their individual needs.

Ceramic package

A SUPERCOMPUTER

This mighty supercomputer does
not use microprocessors to
perform the massive calculations
needed to simulate the behavior
of a nuclear power station – they
are much too slow. But there are
some microprocessors inside. The
computer depends on them to
look after the power and cooling
systems concealed under the seats
that surround it. Without these,
the supercomputer would not
stay up and running.

8237635UAB   247

X

A different way of life

PEOPLE IN THE INDUSTRIALIZED WORLD depend on electronics throughout the day. A quartz clock bleeps a morning alarm, a microwave oven heats a meal, a television set provides evening relaxation. Other electronic systems control air and road traffic, get products onto supermarket shelves, and link a billion telephones. Little of modern life is untouched by electronic technology, yet the rate of development can leave people feeling confused, as the simple and familiar is constantly replaced by the complex and new. This change is tolerated, however, because electronics delivers useful things. Anyone with the right equipment can now take an excellent photograph, quickly call up a friend on the other side of the globe, or even fax them a birthday greeting. Thanks to electronics, consumer goods are better designed and cost less. The workplace is brighter and cleaner, while at home news and sports are flashed from all over the world.

BUILDING CARS
Robots are machines that use electronics (pp. 56-57) to imitate the movements of human operators. They have been used in increasing numbers since the 1970s. Motorists have benefited from their introduction by driving better-made, better-value cars. The workers who remain in the factory are better off, too, because robots now do many of the dull and dangerous jobs.

Cellular phone · Car radio · Hi-fi stereo · Electronic ignition · Engine-management computer · Central locking · Anti-lock braking system · Central locking · Anti-lock braking system

ELECTRONICS IN THE CAR
The basic design of the car has not changed for 60 years, but its electrical and electronic systems have improved enormously. Car radios were available in the 1930s, but electronic systems that were reliable enough to form part of the car itself were a breakthrough of the 1970s. Digital systems can now monitor and control engine and brakes for greater efficiency and safety, besides providing convenient security systems and sophisticated communications equipment.

PORTABLE SATELLITE TERMINAL
This journalist's portable satellite terminal connects his computer to a newspaper office thousands of miles away. The satellite he is using can be accessed directly, rather than through a ground station (p. 13). The microwave signal (pp. 40-41) is sent out by an antenna under the white dome.

Battery compartment at the back

Lid opened to access buttons

Television control
Edit and code setting
Liquid crystal display
Timer and clock control
Number keypad
Teletext opera
VCR control

VCR REMOTE CONTROL
Communicating with electronic equipment can be frustrating. This remote control sends pulses of infrared light to a VCR, which can decode them to tell which key was pressed. But its microprocessor (pp. 58-59) offers so many possibilities that the control's small display is hardly adequate to tell the user what is going on. It represents the sort of electronic technology many people dislike. Some of its features will probably never be used.

he first fax machine was designed
1843. Fax was widely used from
bout 1925 onward for newspaper
ictures and in some businesses from
ne 1960s. But only in the 1980s,
hen ingenious coding systems
sing microprocessors (pp. 58-59)
ad been developed, could a fast,
nexpensive fax machine be built to
ransmit graphic images down
n ordinary telephone line.
feature of fax is its
bility to cross
nternational time lines
nd language barriers.
mages can be sent with
time delay, and the
ecipient can translate
oreign phrases at leisure. Fax
s popular in Japan, where the
vriting system does not lend itself
o other forms of transmission.

Telephone handset

Keypad

Liquid crystal display

brother FAX-160

Documents fed in here to be scanned for transmission

Fax received on thermal paper

THE FASTEST TIME

Electronic technology feeds our
obsession with time. In competitive
sports, records are broken, and
reputations are made. Performances
are measured in milliseconds (p. 23).
There is little point in measuring time
so accurately if other factors are not
taken into account. Electronic
equipment also checks the length of
the track and monitors the
temperature and wind speed.
Electronic analyzers check for the
presence of drugs in the athletes'
blood, and the breaking of a record
is noted in an electronic database.

Sprinter Carl Lewis
winning the 100-meter sprint

SPECIAL EFFECTS

The Walt Disney film *Tron*
(1982) was the first major
production to make
extensive use of computer-
generated special effects.
Earlier, animated films
were laboriously built up
from cells drawn by
armies of artists. They
were limited to images
that could be created
with brush and paint.
   The computer has
opened a new world of
fantasy, not only for
film directors, but also
for the millions who
play video games.
But few technologies
ever disappear
completely. The
sound track on this
print of *Tron* uses a
system invented
in the 1920s.

Frame

Sound track

DEFENSE SYSTEMS

Not the ultimate video game, but a real command
and communication center on an aircraft carrier of
the U.S. Navy. Besides the conventional orange radar
screens (p. 40), it has several computers to keep track
of the data coming in. The increasingly important
field of electronic warfare can both detect threats and
respond to them. But with nothing to see except an
electronic display, how real would the resultant
destruction seem?

The future of electronics

IN THE PRE-ELECTRIC WORLD, change was rare. Printing – the communications revolution of the 1450s – remained fundamentally unaltered for more than 500 years. But electronics began to transform printing in the 1960s, and now, with awesome means of electronic computing and communication at our command, frequent change is the norm in all areas of life. Last year's technology is a museum piece. Companies have become international. Instant, inexpensive communication has intensified competition, while computers have given the power of mathematics to every manager. Electronics itself is not immune to accelerated change. Vacuum tubes (p. 28) dominated electronic technology for 50 years. Transistors, as separate components, gave way to integrated circuits (pp. 52-53) after 25 years. Now, electronics is giving birth to a new technology – photonics. Springing from the technology of fiber-optic communications, photonics promises to control light with light, raising the possibility of future all-optical computers many times faster than their electronic ancestors.

Type locked up to form a page

Block for printing picture

Print made from an inked block

LASER PRINTER
Today, ideas can get from author to reader by a route bypassing traditional printing operations. Keystrokes memorized on a computer disk (p. 57) access another memory that holds the shapes of letters and pictures, driving a laser printer that can put complete documents straight onto paper. A fax machine (p. 63) or direct fax link can create a copy any distance away in seconds.

LETTERPRESS PRINTING
Despite mechanization, printing did not change fundamentally for more than 500 years after its invention around 1450. Lines of metal type were assembled into pages, following the author's manuscript, then inked and pressed onto paper in a press. Image reproduction changed more quickly. Blocks were originally engraved by hand, but by 1900 photographic engraving was common.

Control

Liquid crystal display

Laser-printed document

Paper feed

Printer has its own memory storing letter shapes

A4

FIBER-OPTIC CABLE

Fiber optics began to be important in the late 1970s as the limited capacity of copper cables threatened to throttle the expanding communications network. After attempts to use waveguides (p.41) to link city centers, it was realized that laser light – pulse-code modulated (p. 46) and traveling in hair-fine glass fibers – could offer almost unlimited communication capacity. Fiber-optic links have now replaced cables on most major telephone and data routes.

Insulated plastic covering

Optical fiber

INSTALLING FIBER-OPTIC CABLE

New technologies demand new skills, and workers must adapt or move on. It has taken several years for reliable ways of joining and handling fine glass fibers to be developed. Though the fibers are tough, any kinks allow light to leak out, causing the signal to lose power. To avoid this, fibers can be wafted into ducts, as here, by a stream of air.

UNPLANNED OBSOLESCENCE

Electronic technology ages rapidly. This vacuum tube computer, used for business management rather than scientific calculation, was considered advanced in 1953, but its computing power was comparable to that of a modern programmable hand-held calculator.

COMPUTER-AIDED DESIGN

It used to be difficult to communicate the shapes designers wanted to the people who make the tools that press car bodies out of metal. Now that computers can calculate and specify every point of a three-dimensional curve – here a computer printout is being scrutinized – fashion in car design is changing from a rather boxy look to something much smoother.

CELLULAR PHONE

The telephone was tied down by wires when it appeared in 1876. Now computers have let it off the leash. Cellular phones are possible because a network of radio transmitters can, under computer control, use the same scarce frequencies many times over. Inexpensive phones like this one can only make one-way calls, but by the year 2000 advanced pocket communicators will probably be commonplace.

Earpiece

Liquid crystal display

Keypad

Microphone

OVERSEEING EARTH

Electronics has given us a new world view. Without computers and communications there would be no space satellites. Without satellite pictures, often delivered by electronic technology, most people would not think of their planet as the small and vulnerable place it is.

The invention of printing ushered in a long period in which people thought they could use knowledge to shape the world. Electronics has shown them otherwise.

Index

Acknowledgments

Dorling Kindersley would like to thank:
John Becklake, Stewart Emmens, Stephen Foulger, Ian Carter and Science Museum Library Staff, Brian Gilliam and object handling team, Derek Hudson, Douglas Millard, Peter Stephens, and Anthony Wilson for advice and help with the provision of objects for photography at the Science Museum; Karl Adamson, Dave King, Philip Gatward, and Visual 7 for photography; Printing paraphernalia (p. 62) lent by the John Jarrold Printing Museum, Norwich; Sony and Walkman (p. 53b) are registered trademarks of Sony Corporation, Japan; spectrum analyzer photographs throughout the book by courtesy of Marconi Instruments Ltd; jukebox on p. 56r from RS Leisure Ltd, The Jukebox Showroom, London NW10; printed circuit boards (pp 17 & 23) from Somerville CDO Circuits, London SE16; Gregory Jennings, Imperial College for help with the oscilloscope images; Dixons, London for the loan of electronic equipment on pp. 3r, 4bl, 7t, 41t, 63r; Dr. Bryson Gore and Bipin Parmar at The Royal Institution for allowing us to photograph the wave machine on pp. 14-15; Peter Ramiz and the staff at MESH for computing equipment on pages 45b, 53br, 55br, 57c, 62b; GEC Plessey Semiconductors for objects on p 54b; Olympus for the camera on p. 21b; GEC-Marconi Research Centre for the SAW filter on p. 35t.

Illustrations John Woodcock; Nick Hall; Stephen Bull; Roy Flooks
Index Jane Parker

Picture credits
t=top b=bottom c=center l=left r=right

Allsport 8c; 48tr; 59tc; 61cl. Aquarius Picture Library 46cr. Arcaid 51tr. Associated University Presses/*PaulEisler: My Life with the printed circuit* 23cr. Courtesy of A.T.&T. Archives 31tr; 38br; 49tr. Copyright © BBC 27tr. Bettmann Archive/UPI 40tl; 48br; /UPI 58tr. BT Museum 25tc. BT pictures; a BT photograph 47c; 63tr. Capel Manor 33tl. Colorsport 44tl. Jean Loup Charmet 12tl; 14cl. Mary Evans Picture Library 8tl; 9tr; 20tl; 22cl; 24br; 26c; 42tl; 46tl; 50tl. Ronald Grant Archive 6tr; 9tr; 61tcr. Robert Harding Picture Library 41tr; 43br; 45cl; 60tr. Hulton Deutsche 11tc; 28bl; 36tr; 37tl; 42bc; 63tl. Image Bank 17bl. Imperial War Museum 40bl. Jane's Information Group 61bl. Magnum Photos/Erwitt 20cl. Mansell Collection 19cl; 26tl. Northern Telecom Europe Limited/STC Archives 47cl. Popperphoto 30tr; 30cr; 38tl. Science Museum Library 13c; 29cl. Science Photo Library/Simon Fraser 7tcr; 7cr; 9bcr; 10tr; 13cr; 16tl; 25tl; /P.Parviainen 26br; /Occidental Consortium 28br; /William Curisger 33br; 36c; /Simon Fraser 36bc; 45cr; /Dr Jeremy Burgess 47tl; /Andrew Syred 47tr; Alfred Pasleka 51br; /Manfred Cage 53c; /Takeshi Takahara 54tl; /David Parker 55tl; /David Parker 55bc; /Ray Ellis 55tr; /Jeremy Burgess 56bl; /David Scharfe 57br; /James King Holmes 59bl; /David Parker 59br; /George Haling 63cl; /NASA 63bc.Texas Instruments Ltd 53tc. Zefa 35tl; 59tl; 60l.

With the exception of the items listed above, and the objects on pages 1, 6b, 7b, 11b, 12c, 15b,16l, 17b, 19r, 19c, 21t, 23t, 31r, 34t, 36l, 37r, 38cr, 39c, 40cl, 43b, 46b, 47b, 49b, 50/51c, 56l, 58l, 59t 60b, 61t, all the photographs in this book are of objects in the collections of the Science Museum, London.